MW00649071

## Advance Praise for *Stop Hiding and Start Living*

"Without learning how to fail, we'll never truly flourish. This is the crux of Dr. Bill Howatt's new book, *Stop Hiding and Start Living*. Part mental health primer, part workbook, *Stop Hiding and Start Living* lays out the building blocks Dr. Howatt deems foundational to mental wellness, while reframing life's challenges from pitfalls to stepping stones to growth."

**LOUISE BRADLEY**, C.M., President and CEO, Mental Health Commission of Canada

"Dr. Bill Howatt humbly shares his authentic life story—inspiring readers to take 'tried and true actions' toward achieving fulfilled and happy lives. *Stop Hiding and Start Living* is an honest and direct book of instruction on how to thrive in life."

**ALLAN J. STORDY**, President and CEO, Arete HR Inc.

"Dr. Bill Howatt's passion and commitment to his work is contagious and, with this book, he's providing an extremely practical and actionable approach to getting started on a life-changing journey!"

**LYNN BROWNELL**, President and CEO, Workplace Safety and Prevention Services

"Dr. Bill Howatt seamlessly intertwines poignant and evocative personal narrative with a straightforward and pragmatic toolkit. He brings the theoretical to the personal, and takes you on a journey that will inspire honest self-reflection and effect positive change in your life."

**SAPNA MAHAJAN**, Director,
Treasury Board of Canada Secretariat, Government of Canada

"Dr. Bill Howatt's book is required reading for anyone who is truly looking for the tools that will help them build a balanced life. *Stop Hiding and Start Living* will give the reader the skills needed to achieve this balance."

**GREG HEMMINGS**, award-winning filmmaker and entrepreneur

"Dr. Bill Howatt has spent decades guiding people toward enhanced happiness and well-being. He knows what works. What's more, he's articulate and accessible. Looking for new ways to care for your team? Trying to help someone find their footing? Searching for insights that will reveal new paths on your individual journey? *Stop Hiding and Start Living* will be a beacon of clarity and inspiration that lights your way."

**GREG WELLS**, PhD, CEO of Wells Performance Inc.,
and author of *The Ripple Effect*

# STOP HIDING
# AND
# START LIVING

HOW *to say* F-IT *to*

FEAR *and* DEVELOP

MENTAL FITNESS

# STOP
# HIDING
# AND
# START
# LIVING

*Dr.* BILL HOWATT

●● **PAGE TWO** BOOKS

Copyright © 2020 by Dr. William A. Howatt

All rights reserved. No part of this book may be reproduced, stored in a retrieval system or transmitted, in any form or by any means, without the prior written consent of the publisher or a licence from The Canadian Copyright Licensing Agency (Access Copyright). For a copyright licence, visit www.accesscopyright.ca or call toll free to 1-800-893-5777.

Cataloguing in publication information is available from Library and Archives Canada.

ISBN 978-1-989603-16-1 (paperback)
ISBN 978-1-989603-17-8 (ebook)

Some names and identifying details have been changed to protect the privacy of individuals.

This book is not intended as a substitute for the medical advice of physicians. The reader should regularly consult a physician in matters relating to his/her health and particularly with respect to any symptoms that may require diagnosis or medical attention.

Page Two
www.pagetwo.com

Edited by Al Kingsbury and Amanda Lewis
Cover and interior design by Setareh Ashrafologhalai
Printed and bound in Canada by Friesens
Distributed in Canada by Raincoast Books
Distributed in the US and internationally by
Publishers Group West, a division of Ingram

20 21 22 23 24   5 4 3 2 1

www.howatthr.com

*To my mother*

# CONTENTS

"You can't go back and change the beginning, but you can start where you are, and change the ending."

C.S. LEWIS

# INTRODUCTION: START LIVING

IFE CAN BE wonderful—and life can be wicked.

There can be times in your life when you're happy. You're in love, your children are healthy, and you're professionally fulfilled.

And there can be other times when you worry about how you'll get through. Your finances are a burden, your blood pressure is sky-high, and your relationship is falling apart.

When there are so many moving parts and you don't know where to start, it's hard to create the life of your dreams. Even if you do know what to do to improve your situation, you might be stuck, afraid to take a step because you could fail. This feeling of being stuck is normal; it's designed to help you feel safe. But you can't grow and move to a flourishing state unless you challenge this fear.

As a long-time counsellor, specializing in addictions, I often see clients finally reach a point where they're so unhappy that they say, "That's enough; it's time to move on." In other words, they say, "Fuck it, I'm going to try even if I fail. My happiness is worth it." These *F*-it moments are the intrinsic nudges that help you get out of your own way and start living.

The *F*-it model is a five-part process that can help you face fear directly and move through failure to build a life you love.[1] *F*-it moments occur when you're able to find the determination and motivation to move ahead. Progress may be slow, but even a small change, made regularly, can have huge rewards. The point is to move from low success to a place where you can excel and become who you want to be.

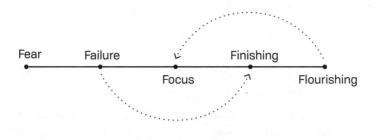

THE *F*-IT MODEL

Let's look at the example of dealing with debt. To apply the *F*-it model, you say *F*-it to *fear* and decide to act regardless of the outcome. Then you're bound to experience some setbacks, or *failure*. But small wins will occur—maybe you pay off a few thousand dollars, or refinance so you have a lower interest rate—and you start to *focus*. You believe that you can pay back the debt and you throw all of your energy at it: packing a lunch instead of eating out, taking on a part-time job to bring in more income. In time, you *finish* what you set out to do: you pay off all your debt. You're now *flourishing* in this part of your life, and you know what daily actions to take to ensure that you stay out of debt. You've developed healthy coping strategies, and as a result, your mental health has improved.[2]

Here's another example. Kelly is forty-five, and at a point where she's starting to be concerned about her career satisfaction. She's been in her job for fifteen years and is used to the work, but isn't feeling the same sense of satisfaction or excitement she once did. Kelly is ready to do something to change her situation, but what if no one hires her? What if nothing improves? *Fear* in this case doesn't imply danger—it refers to the feelings that inhibit Kelly from trying because she's concerned about *failure*.

Until Kelly can work through what fear means to her, she won't be open to the possibility of failure. To fail requires us to try, and in order to try, we need a purpose. Kelly knows that addressing her career satisfaction will result in more happiness, which will also improve her relationships.

Kelly may not quit her job, but she can start applying for other jobs. She makes it her goal to send out a resumé every evening. When she *focuses* on her larger purpose—to enhance her career satisfaction and create more happiness—she has the motivation to keep trying, despite initial setbacks.

Kelly starts to interview successfully and to be offered opportunities for employment. Because she's *finished* the process of trying to get a new job, she finds an opportunity and begins to feel more fulfilled. For the time being, at least, Kelly is *flourishing*. Kelly may not be happy in her new role indefinitely, but the good news is that she can repeat the *F*-it process at any point.

What about your own life? Maybe you can already identify several areas where you're stuck. But where should you start?

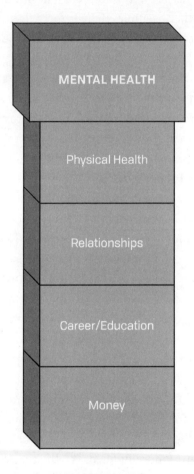

THE LIFE PILLAR

I know it can be overwhelming to change a behaviour or outlook, so I've developed a method for you to compartmentalize your life and systematically address each part, using the *F*-it process. Think of your life as a series of five levels in a pillar.[3] At the bottom are the basic security needs of *money*, then *career* (or education). On top of those levels are *relationships* and *physical health*. Crowning the pillar is *mental health*. Most people focus on the lower levels: money, career, relationships. But all of the lower levels need to support the most important level: mental health. Being healthy in mind, body, and spirit (or emotions) represents a state of total wellness.

Now think of each level in this pillar holding various building blocks. These building blocks support the level, and thus, the whole pillar. Each building block represents a different challenge that needs to be dealt with and managed for the pillar to stand and support its primary function: mental health.

Your *money* level could include the building blocks of savings, debt, and charitable donations. When one or more building blocks don't seem to be correct or positioned the way you want them to be, this can create strain and challenge. Not paying attention to an important building block can also create stress—for instance, ignoring debt can result in personal financial challenges, up to and including bankruptcy. You may not have the capacity to deal with all of the blocks at once. Ask yourself which block is taking most of your attention at this moment. If it's debt, for example, focus your attention there and start taking action to resolve the issue before moving on to another block. In chapter three I'll walk you through the process of choosing a level and selecting a block to work on.

Why go level by level? Because of life's demands and your own priorities, it can be common to spend a lot of time focusing on *money*, *career*, and *relationships*, and not have much energy left over for *physical health* or *mental health*. Moving through each level gives you the opportunity to grow toward positive mental health each day, despite the inherent challenges. By using the *F*-it model to examine one or two building blocks at a time, you can begin to understand how any of the five levels might be out of order, and how all five levels work together in your life.

You may wish to improve in several areas, but it's important to be patient and pick one or two building blocks to start. The more focused and deliberate you are, the more success you'll eventually have. Once you're successful in one area, you can address another building block in that level or apply the *F*-it model to a different level. Bit by bit, making small changes every day, you can act to improve your life.

But what does action look like, when you've been avoiding a particular block or level for months or even years? How can you "unstick" yourself and turn a stumbling block into a building block?

## My Story of Becoming Unstuck

My mother tells me that as a young child I would get up in the middle of the night and go to my little rocking chair. As I sat there rocking, I'd tell myself stories about all the cool things I would do with my life. It appears that I was telling myself what

I *could be*, instead of focusing energy on what I was not. From a young age, I've been driven to create the world I want to live in, an approach that has had a profound, positive impact on my mental health.

But my mental health wasn't always as strong as it is today. I know firsthand the experience of failure. I have dyslexia, and for the first twenty years of my life, I lived in a constant state of fear that I would never be able to advance because I couldn't learn. Every day from grades one to twelve, I worried about failing. In university, a professor noticed I was struggling and helped me put strategies in place so I could finish assignments. I went through a process to fix one building block in my mental health level that was holding me back: my ability to read and write. Small wins gave me the confidence and drive to finish and flourish.

Over time, my mental health evolved from poor to good. I went on to earn seven university degrees and a post-doctorate in behavioural science, and support people with mental illness and mental health issues, including addiction.

Though I didn't develop the *F*-it model until years later, I share my story in this book to show how small actions over time can add up to big achievements. I also share the success stories of clients (with names and identifying details changed) who have implemented the *F*-it process to make big changes in their lives.

## Choose to Be Happy

We all experience stresses and failures. But we can also develop coping skills that will transform even the worst situation into an opportunity to build the mental skill of *resiliency*—the capacity to deal with and push through different degrees of adversity. Many people struggle with their mental health because they've never developed foundational intrapersonal skills, such as stress tolerance, self-direction, and self-awareness. These skills determine how you define, interact with, and process the world. Being able to cope with life's stressors is a key factor in increasing your daily happiness.

You're probably familiar with physical fitness: exercise, rest, and adequate nutrition. But can you recall taking a course that improved your mental fitness? That prepared you to deal with stress and push through difficult times? Not likely. Like most people, you probably haven't been taught how to develop and maintain your mental health. It is not enough to think about being physically healthy—you have to *do* something about it. The same holds true for mental health: you must consciously *act* with intention to improve or maintain your mental health.

If you haven't learned how to manage your mental health, you may be struggling to cope with life's demands. When your resiliency is low, you're at risk of not being able to deal with toxic stress, for example, work demands, unhappy relationships at home, and financial concerns. When this stress becomes chronic, it can have a negative impact on your health and put you at increased risk for mental health problems or mental illness.

Forrest Gump was right when he said about life, "You never know what you're gonna get." Luck, genetics, and your environment certainly play major roles in how your life turns out. But your life evolves because of what you choose to do with what you have.

The sad reality is that many of us are unconsciously checking the boxes with a focus on getting through each day, instead of living each day to its potential. We're caught in a loop of Monday to Friday, week after week, so we're living but not thriving. We haven't learned ways to feel more satisfied and happy with who we are, what we have, what we do, and where we're going. But happiness is fuelled by what you do and what you believe, and it's possible to change your behaviours and habits. The growing field of positive psychology proves that you can learn to be happy, and the degree of happiness can influence how you perceive the world.[4]

When it comes to mental health, you may believe that what you have is it—that it's not possible to shift your habits or change your way of thinking. But like any life skill, maintaining mental health requires knowing what's possible, then learning and practising.

If two people are in the same situation, why does one thrive while the other stays stuck in hopelessness? It's because their perceptions have resulted in different realities.[5] The first person is living in a way in which happiness and success seem possible, even with their current barriers and challenges. The second person feels trapped, with no plan or notion that things can get better. They begin to lose hope by the day, which has a negative impact on their mental health.

They struggle to feel contented or satisfied with their circumstances and to find any happiness.

Mental health is not passive; it's a practice, influenced by what you do and what you think. How you cope with life experiences ultimately shapes your mental health and degree of happiness. Just as daily reps with weights build muscle over time, so small, intentional actions can build mental fitness.

After thirty years as a counsellor, I'm convinced that many of the skills people need to cope with life more effectively can be taught. The earlier these skills are acquired, the better equipped you are to make healthy life choices. This book will help you learn those coping skills.

---

### "Hope is not a plan."

ANDERSON COOPER

---

## Be Aware, Be Accountable, and Act

Happiness and well-being are not destinations; they're an outcome of choices you make, and ways of being and living daily. The key to changing your life and boosting your happiness —no matter what you're struggling with—is to be aware, be accountable, and act.

Part 1 of this book helps you develop *awareness* of the state of your mental health and the other levels in your life pillar. You'll pick a level and a block to focus on. Maybe you're flourishing in your relationships level, but your physical health level needs some attention. You'll learn the differences between "good stress" and "bad stress," and how you can own your story so you can change it.

Each chapter in part 2 unpacks insight into the five *F*s of the *F*-it process, examining behaviour change and habit building—not only in the moment, but long term. We'll consider what lies at the root of fear and failure, and how to make small changes in your life so that focusing, finishing, and flourishing become your usual state.

You'll start to build *accountability* for your outcomes. I'll also give you practical tips and exercises for how to take *action* toward happiness today.

Some people have, without realizing it, created ineffective daily programming. As you move through each chapter of this book, you'll learn how to become your own master programmer to create effective daily programming.

For many of us, change is not easy. Rewards and deep meaning can be the outcome of achieving goals, but not without meeting challenges and having a deep desire to create happiness from within. You can act daily to achieve your life goals, learn how to be happy with who you are, as well as grow and improve your situation.

When it comes to creating positive mental health, many of us don't have a formula. Thankfully, *F*-it offers a path to change your perception and develop your mental fitness.

# 1

# AWARENESS

# 1

# OWN YOUR STORY

WE'LL BE HAPPY only when we define what happiness means to us and acquire the skills to achieve it. Being happy starts by owning our memories and charting our future.

Do you recall your oldest memory? As you ponder, I'll share mine.

Picture a perfect blue-sky summer day. I'm four years old, sitting on a red metal tricycle in front of my childhood home on Brighton Road in Charlottetown, Prince Edward Island. I'm on the sidewalk, backed up to the steps of the front porch of our modest green bungalow. My eyes are directed across the street to a row of trees that edge Victoria Park. Beside me, less than a foot away, is Tammy, a female German shepherd with a perfectly proportioned black and tan face. The two colours weave themselves across her shiny coat with a small patch of white on her chest that you need to be very close to notice. As the wind blows, it appears from my perch that the treetops are painting pictures against the blue sky.

As I happily watch the art show unfold, I feel Tammy's powerful presence. She's a proud dog who always presents herself to me with devotion, kindness, patience, and love. It's only years later that I recognize this memory as representative of a moment in time when I was flourishing as a child: I felt safe and happy. Tammy was my protector who never left my side until she was confident I was okay on my own. She made it possible for me to create and play in safety, and to enjoy the world on my red trike.

I'm grateful that I have this memory to tap into, as not all my early memories are positive. Through my life journey I've learned the benefits of not putting more weight on negative memories than on positive ones.

As you recall your oldest memory and consider where you are today, how similar is your memory to your current state of being?

_____

_____

If your oldest memory is positive, how is your life today? Would you describe it as positive too?

_____

_____

Or is your oldest memory negative and you're still looking for a path to find more positivity in your life?

_____

_____

## Accentuate the Positive

Even when we've been warned that some behaviour is harmful, we often ignore warnings and feel an urge to test the limits before defining something as being not good for us. Am I the only one who knew beforehand that it wasn't a good idea to touch the stove to see if it was hot, or to check whether a razor was sharp by testing the edge against my finger, but still needed to confirm it was unsafe?

Only through life experiences do we learn what is "good" or "bad." Classical behavioural theory, such as operant conditioning, suggests that we learn from our interactions and test with our environment. By touching a hot stove or brushing the edge of a razor, we learn pain and pleasure firsthand. And generally, we seek out pleasure and avoid pain.

If our memories are good, they're easier to explore and discuss; when they're bad, not so much. Whether your oldest memory is a pleasant one, like my red-trike recollection, or something more unpleasant, memories play a role in your mental state. The events you experience and your reaction to them can influence who you think you are and will become.

I've struggled with mental illness over the years, and even with all my training and experience I know that I can't take my mental health for granted; I need to pay constant attention to my thoughts. I've discovered that what I think about is what I will believe to be true, so I've become mindful of the value of positive thoughts about myself and others.

Fortunately, we can train our brains to look at the bright side. Even though the brain is biased toward negative thinking that keeps us safe, it's possible to shift our thinking over time. *Neuroplasticity* is the brain's ability to continuously change. The brain generates neurons throughout our life, a process called *neurogenesis*. It is constantly being shaped by our experiences, thinking, and emotions.[1] New and existing neurons undergo structural and functional changes in their circuitry in response to their environments. Training and experience further enhance this natural phenomenon.

The brain is highly dynamic; it learns what we teach it.[2] Simply put, the way you choose to view things eventually becomes part of who you are. If you train your brain to be negative, it will learn how to find the negative, because it's predisposed to do so. However, it takes the same amount of energy to train your brain to find the positive, and this benefits not only you but also the people around you. The world is an imperfect place, so the more you're able to see things in a positive light, the better your overall mental health will be.

Write out the top five things you're grateful for and why. This activity will remind you of what's positive in your life, which can help you see the world through a hopeful lens.

1.
_____

2.
_____

3.
_____

4.
_____

5.
_____

## Your Mental Map

Your mental map frames what you regard as important and reveals how you view the world.[3] One way to think about a mental map is like a software programming code that defines how you behave daily and predicts how you will react in a situation. When you encounter events that aren't aligned to your mental map, you can quickly become upset and concerned. Often, it's helpful to look beyond your mental map and the triggers that impact how you feel. For example, when you walk into the house after a long day and you see beautiful flowers on the kitchen counter and dirty dishes in the sink, what grabs your attention first, and why?

Some of us, without knowing it, have trained our brains to find the negative: the dirty dishes. An explanation for this is known as *confirmation bias*. Suppose, for example, that you expect that the house should always be kept clean. You walk into a kitchen that's neat and clean, with a beautiful vase of flowers on the counter, but still you focus on the dirty dishes. Ignoring all the good, you say to yourself, "I knew it: the house would be a mess when I got home." This is one example of having trained yourself to look for the negative to confirm your expectation. In a case like this, you may keep looking for more messes.

But focusing on the positive can expand the borders of your focus: beyond the dirty dishes to the otherwise clean kitchen and the flowers. Shaping your mental map to focus more on perceiving the positive in turn impacts what you think, feel, and do. The more you practise looking for the positive, the more you'll find it.

How about you: Is your mental map more positive or negative?

Do particular areas of your life or certain experiences prompt negative reactions? Why do you think that is, and how could you start to shift that outlook?

_____

_____

_____

## You Can Change Your Story

After I was born in Nova Scotia, I was adopted and moved to Prince Edward Island. There are memories, before those of the red trike and my dog Tammy, that are like the hot stove: they hurt, and I don't have a need to explore them in any more detail or to fully understand them. I've learned that they can't be changed; they are what they are. I've concluded that they have something to do with the loss of my biological parents, and they come from a time of fear.

I don't choose any of these as my oldest memory. I've learned how to release them, and they no longer cast a shadow on my mental well-being. But I'm not naive. I know they subconsciously impacted my personality, and even with all my training I still sometimes struggle with trust, affection, and touch. When I become tense about something, if I don't pay attention and notice my feelings, it doesn't take long for old thinking to kick in, triggering insecurity about losing what I have. This is a sign that something is out of balance in my life and there's an opportunity to act.

I've learned how to invite happiness into my life and to cope with my imperfections in a way that allows me to engage in and get joy from the relationships that I value. Like a person who loses a limb and must adjust, I learned over time that I needed to move past thinking or wondering what could have been. Life is lived in the now, and each day is a new opportunity to find something novel and exciting. I still have days that are hard, where I fail. I haven't figured out how to be happy every day, but I have learned to create a weather system that has many more clear days than overcast ones.

Through my academic studies, I learned that I could experience balanced mental health in conjunction with dyslexia and attention deficit hyperactivity disorder (ADHD). I could be happy, feel fulfilled, and flourish in life while having a genetic make-up that presents challenges to operating within a system that values reading and writing as a primary mode of communication.

Today, I choose to look at my early school years as a challenge from which I developed tools and a skill set to move from a state of fear to a way of flourishing. I hold my mental illness as an integral part of my identity. Like a mountain climber who has summitted Mount Kilimanjaro, I'm proud to tell my story to help others. My belief is that when I own my story and share it, I have an opportunity to help other people reshape theirs.

You can change your story with the right information and self-awareness, taking accountability for what you can control and then acting. In order to create a blueprint for mental health, I had to undertake a process of *unknowing*, or questioning my thoughts around my experience. My unknowing process happened for one reason: the information provided in my new environment. My adoptive parents, Lydia and Harold "Red" Howatt, were not interested in focusing on the deck of cards my genetics dealt me. They concentrated on what we could do every day to create a safe environment and to help me learn how to cope with my failures so I could create the memories I wanted.

For me, failure was the norm. For my parents, failure was a part of learning. It took me many years to grasp their simple but distinct concept of failure and the benefit of viewing failure as a point of learning. My parents made it clear that no one is perfect and no one obtains any goal in life without failing. They wanted me to set my focus not just on the fact that I had failed in school or sports, but on the fact that I had tried.

What kind of story are you telling yourself each day? Do you take responsibility for what happens to you, or do you blame external factors?

$\boxed{2}$

# GOOD STRESS
# VS. BAD STRESS

N THE SAME way as owning your story can change your perception of it, how you think of stress can affect whether it's a help or a hindrance. Do you think of stress as positive or negative?

Many of us associate fear, the first *F* in the *F*-it process, with stress. When we have a challenging situation and we're not sure what to do, we can experience negative stress that can freeze us from moving forward. But stress is often misunderstood, and it's helpful to understand how stress can support us to move through fear.

Stress needn't always be negative. *Eustress* is a form of stress that's good for us and is associated with positive feelings.[1] You might experience eustress learning the guitar or starting a romantic relationship. The other type of stress is *distress*. This bad stress comes in many forms, and it can be tied to a specific event or situation: divorce, excessive work demands, job loss, or trying to balance taking care of a loved one with a day job. We may become overwhelmed by the situation and its perceived demands and expectations.

Think of your current stressors. Is there an opportunity to turn any of them from distress to eustress?

_____

_____

## Bad Stress Creates a Failure Loop

Many of us will interpret a situation, such as approaching a person we'd like to get to know better, as being so scary that we avoid it. Out of fear, we perpetuate a failure loop that prevents us from experiencing new joy. When something becomes painful and you fear more pain if you continue, avoidance is one option, especially when you don't have the internal resources or external support to deal with the situation.

Your coping skills and support systems determine how well you manage when experiencing distress. If you see only the stress and then get caught in the emotions, you experience mostly negative symptoms such as sleepless nights, running thoughts, a compulsion to use drugs, or over- or undereating. In this state, you're looking for ways to feel better instead of solving the problem. Bad stress impacts your decision-making, and in some cases, you can become trapped in negative emotions that feed on fear. A person trapped in a period of bad stress can often feel hopeless and worry that the situation will never improve.

The challenge with bad stress is that if it's not resolved, it can accumulate. Over time, all the chemicals involved in a stress response can become toxic to the body and put you at risk for addictive disorders, mental health strain, or even death. Bad stress, whether from home or work, disrupts daily routines that shape your quality of life. If allowed to manifest, bad stress can facilitate negative health outcomes such as neck or shoulder pain, deterioration of the gums, heart disease, cancer, headaches, upset stomach, shortness with family members, anxiety, and depression.[2] It can weaken the immune system, resulting in increased risk for common colds and other illnesses. Distress that results in chronic strain over time can kill by causing strokes or heart attacks.

However, stress at the right level can motivate you to act and to move toward achieving success. Stressful experiences can be transformational and contribute to life-changing behaviours. Researchers have found that experiencing a traumatic event may result in changes in behaviours that are beneficial to physical health.[3]

You can change your focus from seeing a situation as stressful to seeing it as a challenge that must be solved. Treating stress as a challenge and something you're motivated to focus on increases the speed at which you can begin to feel better. When something seems too hard, you can feel overwhelmed, which can tax your ability to cope. You may shut down and perceive the situation as too stressful. However, if a challenge seems too little, you may feel it's not worth focusing on. We seem to do our best when there's enough challenge to capture our interest and we perceive the reward as having value.

Good stress—becoming a new parent, starting a new job, embarking on a new relationship, or training for a marathon—can be seen as a motivator and a test. We're highly motivated to succeed in situations that bring a degree of pressure and challenge. The good things we want in life often require some persistence and drive to push through discomfort or pain. Running a marathon can be an amazing accomplishment, but the fear of not getting across the finish line can be immense—the stress to complete the race can be the fuel that moves you through your fear and across the finish line. With the right level of challenge and purpose, you can push yourself through personal fears to succeed.

Ask yourself whether you have on one occasion or more rationalized a late-night bag of chips or an extra drink at a bar—or whatever indulgence you tend toward—in the name of stress, to escape pain so you could feel good. Most of us, when caught in bad stress, become motivated, like a pleasure-seeking missile, to look for a quick way to change our emotional state. When we feel stress, we want to find a way to stop it and feel good again.

## Take Control

The first step for taking control is to reframe a negative situation so it becomes a challenge that must be solved. Until you solve the situation, the stressful feelings won't go away. This mindset provides an opportunity to focus on what you can do and what you can control, as well as on the choices you want to make.

One action you can take to move past a stressful situation is to accept that you have control over bad stress through the decisions you make to cope with it.[4] For instance, a group of researchers found that new university students who experienced bad stress due to feeling overloaded could be taught to focus on the stress as an opportunity to make changes and achieve their desired goals, an insight that had a positive impact on their well-being.[5]

When you focus on bad stress, powerful emotions can arise that leave you feeling stuck and trapped. To move past the situation, think about what you can *do* to get unstuck.

When have you used stress to your advantage?

When have you moved past stress in a way that improved your situation?

_____

_____

3

# ASSESS YOUR
# LIVING SITUATION

M Y EARLY DAYS of flourishing and failing, and then gradually learning to create more happy days than unhappy ones, led me to develop the life pillar concept with its five levels and the *F*-it model. By looking honestly at my life and considering one by one what levels to focus on and what building blocks I needed to improve, I learned to move through life in a way that led me to flourishing.

Remember Kelly from the introduction? Her levels look like this:

- Money—no issue; good salary
- Career—feeling lost and unsatisfied
- Relationships—excellent and supportive circle of friends
- Physical health—poor exercise and nutrition habits
- Mental health—struggling with depression

Three of Kelly's levels are clearly not in order. She can use the *F*-it model to begin addressing each of them. Kelly starts by concentrating on her career level, and sends out resumés to tackle her fear that no one will hire her. Gradually she starts to focus on landing a new job, and when she does, she flourishes in her new role.

Now it's your turn. Consider each of the five levels in the pillar of your life. Are there any weak points? The purpose of this exercise is to self-evaluate your situation before beginning the *F*-it process, and there are no wrong answers.

· Money—for your personal and business life; without money, it's difficult to exist in our society

· Career/education—in our culture, a career or education is usually the fuel that provides businesses and individuals with the money they need to exist

· Relationships—marriage, parenting, family, community, and peer relationships are of major importance in our society, but these interactions bring many challenges

· Physical health—body strength, cardiovascular strength, flexibility, nutrition, sleep, and lifestyle choices (e.g., how much alcohol you consume in a typical week)

· Mental health—your beliefs (religion/spirituality), politics, personal values, preferences, self-esteem, self-competency, self-acceptance, and emotions

Pick a level in which you want to make some improvements. Now consider the building blocks within that level. Your relationship level, for example, could include three building blocks: your relationship with your parents, dating, and friendships. Pick just one building block that's your biggest challenge and that will benefit most from your attention.

Write down the level and the specific building block you want to focus on. You might want to use a journal so you're not limited by space. Don't worry about how to work past this block at this stage—in part 2 of this book, you'll be guided through the *F*-it model for this level and block.

Level: _____

Block: _____

Now you can begin to move from *decision-making mode* to *action mode*, which starts with personal accountability. That may sound tough, but until you take ownership of your choices and actions, you'll delay moving from fear to failure. Feel free to return to this section as you work through the chapters in part 2.

It's helpful to understand the bigger reason behind focusing on this level and block. What is your purpose in tackling this block in your life?

How will you know you've been successful in tackling this block? What will be the benefits to you and to those you care about?

_____

_____

Think about what's preventing you from overcoming this life challenge. If a fear related to rejection or risk pops up, that means that you've found a fear worthy of your attention. So, what are your biggest fears around tackling this block? How do those fears already negatively impact your thinking, feeling, and behaviours?

_____

_____

What is the most-used behaviour you engage in to cope with these feelings? How does it help you feel better? How does it make you feel worse?

_____

_____

Ask yourself about the impact and cost to you of doing nothing. If you don't make this change, what is the cost to you and to those you love?

_____

_____

_____

As you plan your next steps, take inventory of your knowledge and skills that can help you succeed, or determine what you will need to learn. It's fine if a part of your plan is acquiring the knowledge and skills to carry it out. For example, deciding to go on a new diet sounds simple in theory, if you know what you need to do to achieve the desired outcome. Write down your current knowledge and skills here, and where you know you have deficits.

_____

_____

_____

_____

What will you commit to do to prepare yourself? For instance, you could

- run your plan by a trusted peer
- study other successful people who have accomplished what you want
- take a short course

---

## Change Happens Over Time

I suggest focusing on one thing at a time to increase the speed at which you learn and make improvements. If you want to improve your financial health, for example, concentrate on one area of it until you see results. Allow yourself to get some traction and confirm that you have a workable plan in place and you're making progress before incorporating another building block from the money level.

It's one thing to know what level you would benefit most from focusing on, but what you *want* to focus on might be quite different. It can be a challenge to find the mental energy to focus on what's important.

Focus is ultimately your ability, with intention and purpose, to concentrate on what you want. None of us gets more than twenty-four hours in a day. But constant time pressures, coupled with the demands of daily life and associated stressors, can wear you down and result in poor decision-making. The more you strive to keep up, the more taxing life becomes. In fact, researchers have concluded that time-related stressors and poor coping skills often lead to chronic stress.[1]

If something is unpleasant, a common tendency is to avoid it or push through it quickly, which can distract you from the task at hand: learning the skills you need to achieve more happiness and live each day to its fullest.

I believe that many people are stuck where they are due to their perceptions. They're convinced that they don't have time or energy to do what it takes to move forward. Life is challenging. But with focus, you can reorder your priorities. You can be accountable to yourself and change your thinking and behaviour. Change is possible, but change requires commitment, time, and patience.

Until you can see where you are and what you want, you clarify what defines success, and you're willing to make an effort to achieve your goals, you won't see the outcomes you want. The good news is that when you have knowledge, a plan, and the skills to carry it out, you can develop to your full potential. That's where *F*-it comes in. Success breeds resiliency—when you can manage your emotions and you have a plan and a larger focus, you can see past your failures, realize that there are more possibilities, and then blossom and grow.

The following chapters explore each of the *F*s in the *F*-it model in detail, giving you strategies for addressing your situation and moving through fear, failure, focus, and finishing to flourishing. If you know that you're in a later stage of the *F*-it model for this particular block or level, feel free to jump to the appropriate chapter. But I'd initially encourage you to read all the chapters in order to gain an overview of the process.

Before we move through the model, take a moment to consider what it would mean to "stop hiding and start living" in your everyday life. What would be possible? Which habits would you drop, and which would you adopt?

_____

_____

# 2

## ACCOUNTABILITY

# FEAR

A SMILE CAME TO my face at exactly 3:30 p.m. every day during elementary school. That's when the loud bell rang through the narrow, concrete halls of West Kent Elementary School in Charlottetown.

*Ring, ring, ring, ring, ring.*

It was as if the bell triggered an electric charge that ran through my body, urging me to not waste any time, to move on to a better place. That place was home.

That bell was my cue to exit the building. I responded instantly, like a racehorse when the starting gate opens. At that point in my life, school was like a mental and emotional torture chamber, and the bell announced my blessed escape.

As soon as I walked out the door, I broke into an eight-hundred-yard dash to our house, where I knew my dog Tammy would be waiting for me. Tammy was a guaranteed source of fun. We would play around the yard, creating a new adventure each time. As soon as we were reunited, my fear fell away; it was replaced by a warm feeling of security and freedom. I jumped on my red bike (having traded in my tricycle by now) to begin a new adventure. For a few hours, the day at school and all of its negativity were left behind.

My first year in grade two was painful. I was falling behind each day, and eventually failed the grade. Each day throughout the year, I awoke fearful of what would happen at school that day.

My biggest burden was my interactions with my homeroom teacher, who I believed didn't like me, care about me, or see any potential in me. Whether this was true or not, I don't know—at that time it was my reality. What we focus on and believe, if left unchallenged, becomes true for us.

In my young eyes, this teacher was controlling and all powerful. As I remember, she made it clear that I was to keep my mouth shut and not repeat to anyone what she'd said, as I didn't have her permission to share our interactions. This may be why my parents did nothing to help me in this demoralizing situation. I didn't say anything to them, I suspect, because I didn't want to do anything that could get me into trouble or create more pain. I had enough pain in my life, and I was fearful of what this teacher could do to me. (Though I did know that if she physically hit me or hurt me, then I had to tell my dad. He had made it very clear that if an adult touched me, I was to let him know.)

That was my programming at that moment in my life. It was an odd and confusing place to be, as I think back on it now—I knew that this teacher was hurting me emotionally every day, yet I was unable to share my distress. I prefer to think that she likely had no intention of hurting me. She was of a different generation and had a different mindset. Empathy was not her strength, and as an adult in power she was likely blissfully ignorant of how powerful her words and actions were to a seven-year-old.

I felt that she saw no potential in me and that she based that assessment solely on my inability to read and write with the ease of my peers. She labelled me as someone who could not learn, which meant that my future was dependent on my physical size. I was a big boy, so she told me there was a path for me as good farmhand material. Words matter, and they can stick with us for a long time. This one teacher's words had a profound negative impact on me.

Because of this teacher's words and the struggles I was experiencing, I feared I would never have the life I dreamed of. I would never become a policeman, fireman, or doctor—the aspirations of my generation.

## Fear of Rejection

I was also feeling rejected by my teacher, who I thought was supposed to be there to help me. Our emotions are like the spice we put on food to change its flavour. Emotions impact how we experience life, and rejection is one of the most common emotional wounds that challenge our ability to find happiness.[1] We experience all kinds of rejections in life. Some are minor, such as not being invited to a peer group dinner or not being chosen for a training. Others are more serious: not getting the job you'd really wanted and had worked for years to obtain, being fired from a job and not understanding why, or being dumped by a partner.

Using functional magnetic resonance imaging (fMRI) research, scientists have found that social rejection triggers the same region of the brain as physical pain.[2] That's why rejection hurts so much, and why Tylenol has been found to reduce the effect of emotional pain.[3] It's no wonder that I look back on my school days as painful, and no wonder that people avoid making change for fear of rejection.

As I reflect on my grade two memories, it's like watching the movie *Groundhog Day*. I got up each day with a pit in my stomach, worrying about what would happen at school. It took me ten minutes to walk there, but less than five minutes to run home. On top of the social rejection I dreaded, I worried about how to push through another day of failure and feared that I would never improve. And I was right: grade two was a long year.

Alfred Adler, one of the fathers of modern-day social psychology, taught that we all want to be part of the systems we value. Adler believed that to complete a successful life journey, you must learn to compensate and adjust. He made no bones about it: life can be hard, and we all are internally driven to fit in and find our place in our community and society.[4]

We all know that rejection can be painful and real. It's not just the actual rejection that matters; it's as much what you do to get back on track and learn how to feel accepted, first by yourself and then by your community.

In those moments when you feel rejection, followed by a sense of deep and profound loss that cuts to the bone, Adler taught that there are things you can do to heal and move forward from your emotional state:

1 change internal rules
2 set new personal goals
3 be clear on life purpose
4 practise a healthy lifestyle
5 monitor the five life tasks equally

Adler defined the five life tasks as *friendship, work, love, self-acceptance,* and *spiritual dimension.* These life tasks, paired with Maslow's Hierarchy of Needs, were the basis for my five-level pillar of money, career, relationships, physical health, and mental health.

Adler suggested that each of these life tasks is required for happiness; a gap in any one could be why a person struggles in life. Like Adler, I believe that many people are discouraged— rather than facing a mental illness—and through education, they can find new ways to think about their world. Assessing and monitoring the five levels of your life on a regular basis is one way to move ahead and find happiness. But even as you develop coping skills, it helps to know that as you move away from fear and toward flourishing, failure will be on your path.

## Fear of Failure

Hard as we try, we all fail. And that's normal. To expand on an adage, you can be sure of three things in life: death, taxes, and failure. It's difficult, if not impossible, to be productive and successful without confronting all three. The purpose of fear is to keep you alive, not stop you from reaching your full potential.

Psychologist Robert Plutchik suggested that there are eight basic emotions: fear, anger, sadness, disgust, anticipation, joy, surprise, trust.[5]

When we experience failure, we feel the first four emotions in Plutchik's model—fear, anger, sadness, and disgust. The path to moving through our primary emotions is to believe that better days may be ahead, and with those days come more positive emotions such as anticipation, joy, and trust.

As an elementary school student, I wanted to learn, but I had days when I was distracted, disruptive, and talked too much. It seemed I was always standing in the hall outside the principal's office or my classroom, depending on the severity of the misdemeanour.

I knew something was wrong, but I was not sure what. At age seven, I had no frame of reference that would enable me to articulate what I was experiencing, nor did I really talk about my daily fear with anyone other than Tammy. I was a quiet, shy kid who felt socially awkward, especially when I was trying to read other kids' intentions when they teased me. One challenge for people with ADHD is to accurately read social cues. This was a real difficultly for me, as I never knew when a peer was tormenting me or "merely" teasing me. So I used the safe approach: I assumed the worst and pushed back.

In the 1970s, few teachers really understood learning disabilities and ADHD, so it wasn't unusual for children like me to be deemed lazy, bad, or dumb, or to be told we had behavioural issues. Much later I learned that learning disabilities and ADHD are classified as neurological disorders within a medical definition of mental disorder or mental illness.[6]

Back then, there were not a lot of support systems for students with dyslexia and ADHD, but my parents did try to find some. They took me to Halifax, Nova Scotia, where skilled doctors at the Izaak Walton Killam Hospital for Children (now the IWK Health Centre) first diagnosed my dyslexia. This information helped my mother understand why I was struggling to learn, but it was difficult to determine what supports I needed or how to help me deal with my emotions and my reality, namely, that I was failing. Since Mom was super-resilient, instead of getting too upset, she decided to figure out what could be done to help me. My mother became active in the learning disability association to help discover what resources could help students like me. All of this love and caring were wonderful, but they didn't change my day-to-day reality in grade two.

Fear of failure can hold us back from trying because of the perception of pain.[7] I had an anchor—my home, my family, and my dog—that helped me know that even if I failed at school, I had a place in my life where I was not a failure. I was set up for success; I just didn't know it. I had love, safety, and protection; between Tammy and my father, nobody was going to harm me. My mother spoke to me every day about where I was going, not where I was or had been. But my reality, as I perceived it, was that I was moving every day from danger to safety and back to danger.

Because I found moments where I didn't have to be a failure, I didn't allow all the pain I was enduring to define who I was. Your environment doesn't necessarily define you, but it does play a role, so it's important to step back to determine whether you're getting the kind of support you need from the environment you choose to live in. Your perception of your environment is defined by the limited processing of observed information. On average, the brain receives eleven million bits of information every second from the environment; however, it's equipped to process only fifty bits per second.[8] As a result, what you focus on defines your reality, which is clearly not the full picture.

It takes awareness to understand that what you observe—whether it's the good parts or the parts that you fear—may not represent the full picture.

## Address the Fear That's Holding You Back

Fear can come in all degrees, from mild to severe, and it can provide an opportunity for new learnings. It's how you cope with these experiences that determines whether you're able to move forward.

In theory, a person could be flourishing at work and failing in their personal or romantic relationships. What stops some people from fixing their relationships is fear associated with the possibility of separation or divorce and its associated consequences. This fear creates a stress level that, if not dealt with, can erode a person's confidence to the extent that they're unsure what to do. They become almost frozen in time, and before they know it, years have passed. They lack confidence in their ability to create a situation that's better than the one they are currently in—thinking it's better to deal with the devil they know than the devil they don't.

Fear is a powerful emotion that has the positive effect of protecting us from physical and emotional danger, but it can also keep us back from trying new things.[9] This latter type of fear can hold you in almost a suspended state of animation, where you become stuck due to internal mental programming that sets the risk tolerance of making a mistake to almost zero. You stick to routines and do all you can to avoid making a mistake or failing, which drastically shrinks your world and opportunities for new growth.

How are you using fear to hold yourself back from making positive change in your life?

As we discussed in chapter two, most bad stress is directly associated with some perceived fear. If you can deal effectively with fear, you can experience more eustress than distress, and have the courage and opportunity to fail. Of course, all of this is easier said than done. Fear can be confusing, as it can happen outside awareness. Every day in grade two, I was feeling stress that was pure fear. I wasn't afraid of failure; I *knew* I was failing. I was afraid that I would never learn.

To move past fear, it's helpful to understand how our brains work. We have a wonderful survival mechanism, which is most likely why we're at the top of the food chain, but also why we have evolved to have so many mental health challenges. When we're exposed to intense, stressful situations of real or perceived threat, our primitive, in-born fight-or-flight response system switches on. This automatic system immediately goes to work to take evasive action to help us escape from perceived harm, danger, or threat.

Physiologist Walter Cannon first pointed out how the fight-or-flight response is a genetic evolution that resulted in the human body creating an automatic radar that's constantly scanning for danger to avoid bodily harm.[10] This survival mechanism protected us from larger species, like sabre-toothed tigers. We used it to fuel our development of tools such as spears and guns, becoming the hunters rather than just the hunted.

One challenge with the fight-or-flight system is that it hasn't evolved or changed. Our brains react the same way and drop the same amount of chemicals when the switch is turned on, whether by the sight of a tiger or the sound of a screaming child. Once activated, the fight-or-flight response delivers adrenaline and other stress hormones directly into the body.

When faced with a personal threat or the fear of losing a loved one, the mind and body can override perceived limits and we can do more than we ever expected. Researchers like kinesiologist Vladimir Zatsiorsky suggest that the average person uses only 65 percent of their muscle potential, whereas a trained weightlifter uses 80 percent. However, under intense, stressful situations, where weightlifters have trained themselves to take more risk, they can perform up to 92 percent of their potential.[11] Many stories of the fight-or-flight response providing the internal chemistry and drive to protect a loved one can be found by googling "mother lifts car to save child."

In a time of intense need and crisis, fear can keep us alive. But for a person who isn't aware of the value of fear, it can be a barrier to moving forward. The brain is on a constant lookout for danger, so the fight-or-flight system stays active; it is always running in the background. When we perceive a threat, the system kicks in, like an octane-booster tank in a car. Once the tank is turned on, the car gets increased power that boosts its performance for a short period until the tank goes dry. The body works in a similar manner. The fight-or-flight response can remain intense for a period, but once the body burns its reserves and has no more energy, it shuts down.

Though this system can be helpful for short periods, if it becomes stuck in the "on" position, it can have a negative impact on your health. For example, if you're living in fear of losing your job, this signals to the body that there's danger. The brain pumps chemicals to protect itself and to generate energy that's not needed. When the fight-or-flight system is engaged repeatedly, the body builds up excessive levels of stress hormone. Failure to metabolize the buildup may be a contributing factor to disorders such as chronic fatigue, depression, lupus, allergies, autoimmune diseases like rheumatoid arthritis, or even the common cold.[12]

We're not just machines that turn on. We have choices, and we must know how to act on them.

## Escape the Fear Trap

When we learn and understand the basics of the fight-or-flight mechanism and how this genetic programming was developed to protect us from real threats, we're able to look for ways to keep it calm when it's not needed. Within a few days, weeks, or months, most of us are able to dissociate from tragic events we read about or watch on TV. How we do this is perhaps due to our ability to compartmentalize and focus on our day-to-day life and actions.

In our culture, it's not the big threats as much as the daily grind of life that creates most, or at least much, of our bad stress. My 2015 research with the *Globe and Mail* found that nearly 60 percent of employees in the Canadian workforce go to work each day experiencing bad stress that comes in many forms: fear of failure, fear of being bullied or harassed, fear of losing a job, and fear of going bankrupt. These are just a few examples of the stressful fear traps that lie in our path in the normal course of the day.

The *fear trap* is the term I use to describe getting caught in a cycle of bad stress that turns on your fight-or-flight system when it's not needed. It can be frightening to get stuck in the fear trap unprepared, without proper insight, knowledge, or support. Over time, the fear trap can trigger feelings of hopelessness and helplessness. Some people can get caught in a fear trap in one of the five levels to the point that they become stuck for an extended period or give up trying. Fear of failure or the loss of hope can paralyze a person and prevent them from ever trying. Sometimes being caught in this fear trap can bring such pain that they look for short-term ways to relieve it that are not in their best interests, such as eating too much, drinking alcohol or taking drugs, or gambling.

Some people come to my office wanting help because they're caught in a fear trap that's having a negative impact on their life and mental health. They want the pain to stop and they're looking for help and guidance. These folks don't have a mental illness; they're simply discouraged and feeling challenged, because they don't know how to stop or resolve the bad stress. The good news is that they believe there may be a different way and have made a positive choice to look for options to solve their challenge, rather than taking a drug to mask it.

Most clients who show up for an appointment on their own steam (rather than being sent to me by a loved one or a health practitioner) are experiencing some level of dysfunction that's having a negative impact on their thinking, emotions, and behaviour. Many are experiencing a mental health problem but don't meet criteria for any mental illness (as defined by the *Diagnostic and Statistical Manual of Mental Disorders*). Most have some underlying fear and are looking for support to move past it and other challenges so they can get back on a positive track. They're discouraged and need to regain emotional control by learning how to solve their challenges, so they diagnose themselves based on various signs and symptoms.

If you have strained mental health, it doesn't mean you have a mental illness or are mentally weak. It means that you're human, trying to process and deal with what's in front of you. Mental health is like the weather; it can change by the hour. The more you learn to cope, the more you can control the mental forecast. Stress, fear, mental health, and mental illness are all interconnected. The more you're aware of those links, the more you can make good choices to solve the challenges you face.

Moving from *fear* to *failure* is the first stage of the *F*-it model—when you have your goals in sight and have acquired enough coping skills to say, "*F*-it! I'm going to try even though I'm afraid." I'm often asked how long it takes to move from fear to failure, where fear no longer holds you back from accomplishing what you want. There's no standard answer; it depends on the situation, what you're trying to achieve, and your level of hope. The right answer is, "As long as it takes!"

## Hope Is an Antidote to the Fear Trap

Hopeful people tend to focus on what's good in their world and they're more likely to find the energy to push through their day as they see opportunities. In the absence of hope, we have nothing. We can all retrain our brain to find positives once we discover that this is an option.

The lens through which you see the world influences what you believe is possible. When you're caught in a fear trap that magnifies hopelessness and feeds your fear, internal conversations can become intense, overwhelming, believable, and painful. The risk is losing your belief that things could ever get better, resulting in negative thinking, up to and including suicidal thoughts. In this mental state, you're unable to debate the terrible thoughts that roll through your head.

However, knowing that there's a fear trap doesn't mean there are no solutions. Your mind can be like a car that doesn't start and do what you want. When your car breaks down, it likely just needs a mechanic to make a tweak or minor repair such as replacing a battery. I don't know how to fix a car, but when there's a problem, I know I need to call a mechanic.

Mental health can be the same. Just because you don't see a solution doesn't mean there isn't one. It can be helpful to know that if you ever get stuck, you can talk to someone like a mental health professional to ask for help. The more you can promote help-seeking behaviours in times of need, the greater your potential for getting out of a fear trap that may be putting your mental health at risk.

Hope is an incredibly important currency, as it pays the entry fee to a world of possibilities. When we have hope, we're positioned to see past fear. Though the path may be long and hard, we still see it. Becoming hopeless can discourage us from doing things we once enjoyed and found rewarding.[13] Hopelessness is an important emotion. When it becomes chronic or intense, it can be one of the biggest predictors of suicide risk[14] and can keep us trapped in fear.

I know that I had many sad days when I was full of uncertainty—even moments when I lost hope. What kept me going was my mother's steadfast belief in my ability to learn, and teachers along the way who shared that confidence. Perhaps if I didn't have a daily action plan of hope—getting home to see my dog Tammy—I might not have gotten to where I am today.

Taking it day by day is the best way to get through. One of my clients, Laura, knows this firsthand. At age forty-two, Laura got the devastating news that she had breast cancer. But from that moment, she spent every breath focused on living, instead of worrying about dying. Laura faced the reality of her mortality much earlier than she'd wanted or expected, but she decided to smile and to look cancer directly in the eye. Her drive was her two young children. She vowed to live as healthily as possible and to fight cancer with every bit of energy she could muster. Within thirty days of her final treatment, Laura completed her first spartan race—an amazing accomplishment. Laura's doctor tried to tell her that even if she beat the cancer, her world would be diminished. Laura rejected this information and decided she would use cancer as a motivator to become the best version of herself. Today, Laura is a beacon of hope and inspiration. She is one example of many people I have met over the years who pushed through their fear to flourishing.

Researchers like Charles Richard Snyder have studied[15] how hope can have a positive impact on our overall health and our belief in what's possible. Snyder suggested that hope can evolve when we have a plan in mind, we are committed, and we execute the plan to achieve a goal. He and his colleagues defined hope as "a positive motivational state that is based on an interactively derived sense of successful (a) agency (goal-directed energy) and (b) pathways (planning to meet goals)."

## Choose Happy Every Day

Hope doesn't need to be passive; it's better to be active in creating hope. Happiness is the same. Happiness is not something that happens after we achieve goals or get some reward. One study compared twenty-two major lottery winners to a group of twenty-nine paralyzed accident victims to determine which group was happier. No real difference was found in the two groups with respect to happiness.[16] It's not what we have in life that brings joy; each of us defines what makes us happy. We get to choose happy every day, and hope creates a crack for happiness to get in.

Psychiatrist William Glasser, who developed choice theory, taught that life happiness is defined by the choices you make. When accepted, learned, and internalized, this insight can be a major step to finding hope and achieving happiness, as you accept that what you think and do impacts your sense of well-being.

Happiness is rooted in two key elements: positive emotions and life satisfaction. Together they create subjective well-being.[17] While most people pursue happiness, the challenge lies in determining just what that state of mind is for each of us. Many people equate happiness with achievement and unhappiness with a failure to achieve goals. But as I like to put it, we don't get happy by getting stuff; we get stuff by learning how to be happy.

Happiness doesn't need to cost anything; it's a frame of mind and a focal point in our lives.

When we have both hope and happiness, benefits await: increased resiliency, quicker bounce-back from negative emotions, being more accepted and liked by others, improvements to the immune system, longer life, and increased self-esteem.

Research indicates that three factors collectively define how much happiness we can experience: life circumstances (environment/networks of support), intentional activities, and genetics.

- Life circumstances: Whether you are married/single, healthy/unhealthy, rich/poor, employed/unemployed, and so on. Many people believe that their situation or environment defines their happiness. Though some benefits can be derived from the environment, it alone doesn't provide long-lasting happiness.

- Intentional actions: The actions you engage in with purpose and intent to determine your degree of happiness. These include well-being activities, developing personal coping skills, creating healthy social networks, performing rewarding work, and supporting your local community through volunteerism.

- Genetics: A set point that varies from person to person and is thought to account for 50 percent of happiness.

*Epigenetics* is a relatively new branch of science. It indicates that how effectively a person learns to cope, think, and feel within their environment can have an impact at a genetic level.[18] This new research suggests that our genetics may not be as fixed as we once thought, meaning that perhaps more than 50 percent of our happiness can be affected by intentions. There's growing evidence that we can determine our happiness through our thoughts, attitudes, and feelings.[19] The upshot is that the better you can learn to positively affect your thoughts, the more you can positively affect your genetics. This, in turn, can influence how you feel, and even your overall well-being and happiness.

By consciously shifting thinking from doubt and fear to positivity, you can influence your state of well-being and come to see your cup as half full. By shifting your thinking to focus more attention on finding what's good, you can increase your optimism, which is the belief that things will work out. Developing optimism can be a major step toward learning to experience more happiness.

## Make the Decision to Act

The first step in the *F*-it process is often the most difficult. Moving from *fear* to *failure* requires you to dig deep and find hope that things can be better. Fear can be an immobilizer, comparable to a car being stuck in park. You must shift into drive to move down the path to *flourishing*—your ultimate destination. For fear to be left in the rear-view mirror, you must give yourself permission to try, knowing that there's a likelihood you'll fail. Once you determine to move forward, making behavioural change may not be as difficult as you think. However, as the driver, you must be clear about what motivates you.

Most of us, when caught in fear, will likely have some experience with hope and happiness to draw upon. The quest for hope can be a motivator to move from the fear that holds you back from giving yourself permission to fail. The aim is to build hope to move from idea to action, knowing full well that you may fail. It's not uncommon for people with low self-worth to feel as if they're not in control of their life circumstances, and many engage in at-risk behaviours (e.g., drinking) to feel better. The root cause of how they got trapped in this behaviour can be directly related to a fear of more failure.[20] They numb themselves, live for the moment, and put their fears and pain at bay. Moving through fear often is dependent on accepting that failure is part of the equation, while having hope to see a better outcome.

Keep in mind that knowing you're stuck in fear doesn't mean there's no hope. When you don't know the answer or feel overwhelmed, it can help to talk it over with a trusted person. If that doesn't help, you can discuss your situation with a mental health professional such as a career and family assistance counsellor.

---

**"I learned that courage was not the absence of fear, but the triumph over it. The brave man is not he who does not feel afraid, but he who conquers that fear."**

NELSON MANDELA

---

## Hope Is the Trigger

Hope begins with a belief and a desire for a better outcome. It's helpful to find motivation to discover hope and make change. One motivational breakthrough from my own experience stands out. It was my sophomore year at Acadia

University. I was playing football for the varsity Axemen, a team with a proud history that included two recent national championships.

When I graduated grade twelve, I felt like it was the end of the line as far as school was concerned. But I could play football well, so I thought I might get to play as a job. I just had to get through university somehow. I didn't think about that part as much as about getting in shape for tryouts. That was something I could control, and I did it well. Playing football was a big deal for me; it gave me an identity. Sports helped me fit in and have a purpose and motivation to keep trying so I could be a part of the team.

But at the end of my sophomore year, things were not going well for me. I was fearful that I would never get to be a starter.

You need to memorize a lot to play football at the university level, learning many plays and poring through thick playbooks. In my first year, I couldn't learn the plays well, since I couldn't read and study at the level required to understand the concepts. The stress and shame, coupled with the low expectations I had for myself, had me on the verge of quitting the squad. These negative thoughts were rolling around in my head, but I wasn't sharing them with anyone. I just didn't know where to go. I felt overwhelmed and insecure, worried that I didn't have the talent to play at such a high level. I was haunted by the fear of another failure.

It was in this make-or-break period that an interaction with a teammate changed everything. Our spring football camp was about to get under way. I wanted to be more than a benchwarmer, but I wasn't yet physically strong enough—or good enough of a player—to earn a starting spot. At this point, the teammate, a fellow non-starter with a high opinion of himself, asked, "What position are you trying for next year?" I replied, "I'm going to try out for left tackle." He began to laugh, and said, "Impossible. It'll never happen. Look at yourself, you're not big enough, good enough, or strong enough."

I said nothing, but that was the trigger I needed to muster the courage to show him he was wrong and I could start as a left tackle. That was my *F*-it moment. I knew that I had to summon the hope to move forward. His criticism moved me to create an action plan for success. His taunting words sparked me to stop worrying about failing and to put all of my focus on proving him wrong. I decided then and there: If I fail, fine, but I'm giving it my very best shot.

It may seem incredible that a casual, five-second exchange could have such an impact, but my teammate's words provided the fuel that gave me the hope I needed. I tapped into that energy source every day as I trained. I had finally turned a corner and accepted that I could fail. I spent the entire summer working on my training and nothing else, completing all my programs and achieving all my training goals. When I entered pre-season camp, I was still stressed and worried about failure, but my hard work paid off. Within a few days, I was named starting left tackle. I had attained my goal and gotten on track to flourishing—and the more I flourished, the more confidence I gained. Not only had I become a starter, but at the end of the season I was named most improved player.

I never thanked that person for the gift he gave me, but that's what it was: a gift. Without it, I might not have dug down and found the hope to push myself forward. Though I felt stressed and hurt at the time, I turned his negative statement into a positive, through my desire to prove him wrong.

While fear and stress can hold us back from trying, hope can push us forward. We're not always going to have such a dramatic set of circumstances to trigger *F*-it moments, but we can create those moments for ourselves.

Personal growth seldom comes without some degree of trauma, pain, or adversity. Consider for a moment that you're Laura and you've just found out that you have cancer. It may be difficult to know exactly what you would do. We know from studying human beings that, when faced with a life challenge, people have no choice but to do something—and what you do will influence how well you're positioned to manage your fear and to push through it. The good news is that the motivation to push through can come from within—Laura didn't need anyone to tell her to fight. Motivation can also come from external sources—being open and listening to the cues, like in my football story, can be the spark to move forward. I'm not sure I would have gotten to the level I did if I didn't have the spark. Hearing my teammate's opinion motivated me to focus on being the best I could be, and to put fear in the rearview mirror.

You can increase your odds of success by accepting that the process of moving from one step to the next is a journey, and set expectations accordingly. Using lessons from life-changing events (e.g., unexpected illness) and developmental challenges (e.g., leaving home to go to university) can be a powerful way to access the courage that's necessary during those times. You can get through a difficult patch and experience personal growth, thereby turning a stressful situation into a new opportunity.[21]

## Create a Success Framework

Even with your best planning, failure can, and likely will, happen. At the beginning of chapter three, you were asked to choose a level of your life pillar and a building block within that level to focus on. Now, using no more than five points, map out the most important steps you believe can lead you to success in your chosen level and building block, thereby reducing your risk of failure. For each action, be specific with respect to its frequency, duration, and intensity.

Ensure that you're taking *calculated* risks, meaning you are considering the potential for risk in your decision-making. This includes considering potential consequences, intended or otherwise. For example, if you want to pay off debt, that might mean you can't attend the theatre or play a sport you enjoy. The risk could be feeling like you'd lose contact with a group of friends. Because of your financial situation, you've decided that for the short term, this is one consequence you may accept so you can achieve your goal.

Ensure that you're taking a well-thought-out step and not allowing blind emotion to push you forward. Be clear on what you'll do by mapping the action steps for the plan, and then stress-test it to ensure that it doesn't carry any unnecessary risks.

## Action plan (max. 5 steps)

1. 

2. 

3. 

4. 

5. 

## Frequency (daily, weekly, monthly)

## Duration (for six months, a year, two years)

## Intensity (on a scale of 1 to 7)

## Possible risks (max. 5)

1. _____

2. _____

3. _____

4. _____

5. _____


## "Go" time—when and where you'll begin your action plan

_____


## Monitor progress

Define how you'll measure and monitor each step. A daily journal is an effective way to organize your thoughts and measure your progress.

_____

_____

_____

If you're afraid of starting, review the sections earlier in this chapter on the fear trap: "Escape the Fear Trap" and "Hope Is an Antidote to the Fear Trap." Don't allow fear to hold you back—use the hope of a happier life to drive you forward to create change every day.

# 5

# FAILURE

I HAD JUST FAILED grade two.

I was sitting alone on one of the red sandstone rocks that adorn the coastline of Prince Edward Island, the Canadian province that Lucy Maud Montgomery introduced to the world through her Anne of Green Gables series.

I watched as the pale blue skies gradually transitioned to haunting grey and then black. The air cooled, and the light breeze that had been blowing off the choppy waters of Charlottetown Harbour turned to gusting winds, producing whitecaps and pushing waves against the shore.

On this suddenly blustery day, I sat and gazed at the ocean, a few feet below the spray of the crashing waves. I watched as if in a trance as the water whipped the shoreline with increasing rage.

In Atlantic Canada, weather can change with little notice, but even at this young age I recognized the signs Mother

Nature gave off when she was about to assault the island. My parents' home had an ocean view, only a hundred yards from where I was sitting, and as I gazed out beyond the harbour, I knew that rain was approaching within minutes. But the threat of getting soaked didn't motivate me to move; I was still processing the news that I had failed grade two. I sat quietly, but my stomach was churning and my heart was beating fast. My mind swam with emotions, from shock to denial, from anger to sadness. I felt confused, unsure what to do or how to cope.

The weather seemed to mirror how I felt inside, yet the growing storm was starting to have a soothing effect. I didn't mind the cold, the wind, the darkness; it was as if I had an ally to help me express my mood and give vent to my feelings.

The news of my failure had been overwhelming. It had immediately become the centre of my small universe. I retreated to this place of comfort I had visited countless times before to escape and seek solace. I stared beyond the harbour to the open ocean, as if searching for answers or perhaps a glimpse into my future.

I wasn't fearful for my physical safety; I knew that if I needed her, my dog Tammy would be at my side in seconds. If I wasn't home on time from school, it wasn't uncommon for her to go looking for me.

Looking back, I realize that this was my first existential crisis. I was experiencing anxiety about my future like I never had before. I was in a bubble, surrounded only by my thoughts, trying desperately to unpack the consequences of my failure.

Failure can happen suddenly, without warning, and it can have prolonged and lasting effects. Failure provides an opportunity for learning, but only when we're ready to learn. When we're not ready, the impact of failure can be magnified. I wasn't ready.

If we're not careful, failure has the power to turn the tables and define us. As a child, I certainly didn't understand my mental health issues. I simply thought I was slow-witted and incapable of learning. I was unaware that if this mindset continued, it could be harmful to my well-being and cloud my future.

Environmental factors aren't everything, but they can contribute to our sense of success or failure. When we look at someone's behaviour and performance in school, it's common to assume that internal factors such as IQ are at play and to underestimate the influence that external factors can have. Psychologists call this a *fundamental attribution error.*[1] At age seven, I had already fallen victim to this destructive thinking. It had been created and projected by my teacher and reinforced at school by groupthink. I started to believe that I might never be able to learn, and this latest failure proved that the teacher was right.

## Normalize Failure

The importance we attach to success and the pain we attach to failure can influence our perception of the degree and magnitude of a failure. In his 2005 book *Blink: The Power of Thinking without Thinking*, Malcolm Gladwell noted that people who master a specific area of expertise are able to make quick decisions within that narrow realm of knowledge. He calls this "thin-slicing," a process that requires years of experience, training, and knowledge. Achieving this point requires focus, time, effort, and the ability to overcome failure.

What course of action, if any, have you taken that allowed you to practise failure in a controlled environment? Most of us are not open to falling short at any stage of trying. We prefer to believe that there's a path to mastery or life success without this misstep. Unfortunately, there's no such shortcut or detour around failure. Once we encounter failure, however, a series of signposts can get us back on the right path.

How you deal with your failures can impact how you define yourself and influence your perspective on life and its meaning.[2] Accept the reality: It's impossible to get through life without failure; moreover, there's really no learning without it.

Is failure in and of itself the issue, or is it the context and expectation we set around failure?

"Ever tried. Ever failed. No matter. Try again.
Fail again. Fail better."

SAMUEL BECKETT

Failure is not only a component of success, it's a vital one. However, without a frame of reference to normalize failure, the very prospect can immobilize you, preventing you from taking another risk and trying again. This mindset creates a mental anchor that prevents you from moving forward, a concept called *learned helplessness*. Learned helplessness is an internal belief system developed by a person who has been unable to escape a painful situation. The individual has determined that there's no escape from the pain and therefore no point in trying. Their conclusion is that nothing they do matters.[3] But with proper support and knowledge, you can avoid this consequence.

Without the support of my mother, I could easily have concluded that I was incapable of learning and remained stuck in fear. Based solely on my daily failures to learn and my flunking grade two, I would have been left believing that there was no hope, no sense of trying anymore. Learned helplessness erodes a person's belief about the future being anything other than the present.[4] Luckily for me, I had a mother who convinced me that failure is okay and that it's one step closer to success.

Our individualistic culture promotes the notion that to get ahead we must always get credit for our success. But really, it's not that clear-cut. In my clinical work, I've found that when a person has a major life failure, their ability to overcome it isn't based just on luck, IQ, emotional intelligence, or hard work. It's the combination of all of these, as well as a healthy network that provides encouragement and support.

When clients who don't have positive support networks experience repeated failure, they're more prone to developing learned helplessness. This can make it hard for someone who has experienced a failure to accept any encouragement or support. Instead of trying again, they may engage in poor coping behaviours to feel better. Eventually, they start to believe that these behaviours, similar to addictions, are in their best interest.

*Cognitive dissonance* can be observed when we simultaneously hold conflicting thoughts.[5] For example, someone might become a smoker and know it causes cancer, but rationalize it as being helpful to calm their nerves. Leon Festinger, who developed cognitive dissonance theory, noticed that people are driven to maintain cognitive consistency. We look for internal harmony that can accept irrational thinking, so that we can rationalize and enjoy risky behaviours such as smoking.

Context is everything. What we believe and what we think others believe defines our perceptions around failure. People who have never experienced failure feel its impact more strongly and are ill equipped to learn from it. They can allow failure to define them. But people who have experienced failure in the regular course of living are less likely to allow this to happen.

It comes down to rules and preferences. People who create an internal rule that no failure is allowed—that they must be perfect—are less likely to cope well when failure inevitably occurs. Conversely, those who are willing to take risks and fail are more likely to dust themselves off and try again, with renewed focus. While everyone prefers success over failure, those who are willing to risk failure can accept it as part of personal growth, and focus on hope and ways to succeed next time.

## Pay Attention to Your Learning Curve

When organizations or parents don't tolerate failure, they stifle human potential. On the other end of the continuum, not recognizing that failure is a part of life can also have a negative impact on a person's development. In a college or university setting, two constructs that create false expectations are grade inflation (instructors feel pressure to give high marks because students expect them) and social advancement (students feel that if they get into the right school, it will set up their future). Inflated grades lead graduates to believe they possess competencies and skills that they do not. This truth is soon discovered in the workplace, where it can result in greater risk for bad stress. Inflated grades threaten to rob the academic marking system of its integrity.[6] When students graduate and enter the work world, they quickly learn that no one is asking them about their grades anymore or where they went to school. They feel pressure to perform, and they risk failure because they may not be as ready as they perceived. Bad stress follows as they try to catch up and learn new skills on the job—where the learning curve is too steep.

It can take knowledge workers, for example, nine months to a year to acquire the core competency, experience, and skill to perform their assigned tasks independently. During any learning curve, the risk for mistakes is high. With new hires accustomed to scoring high marks in university, the impact of failure is worsened. So neither employee nor employer benefits from this well-intended but unhelpful teaching model.

Many organizations make use of mentors and peer support to assist individuals through their initial learning curve, and thereby mitigate the risk of failure. That's why in a critical function such as medical care, two doctors must be present with a patient until the junior doctor has proven their competency.

Research shows that we typically pass through four stages of competency when we are learning something new. Starting out, most people are unaware of how much work it takes to learn a new skill.

Psychologist Albert Bandura's four-step core learning model provides a frame of reference that can help set realistic expectations on the time and effort it will take to master a skill. When you're moving through these four steps, it's helpful to know where you are on your learning curve and accept it as a normal part of the learning process.

1 Unconscious incompetence: You haven't yet discovered, or are unaware, that a skill or knowledge gap exists.

2 Conscious incompetence: You become aware of your skill or knowledge gap, and consider the value of gaining the knowledge and skills to perform the targeted tasks. At this stage, learning begins, but the risk of failure is highest too.

3 Conscious competence: You're now able to practise the skill or perform the task, but doing so requires repetition, conscious thought, and effort. You've moved from dreading failure to accepting that failure is part of the process.

4 Unconscious competence: You've practised and you have enough experience with the skill that you can perform it easily on demand. It's become an unconscious act, like tying your shoes. You've had success and have proven that you can perform the skills successfully over and over.

Most learning curves move through the same basic process, but the complexity of the skill affects the duration and frequency of failure. Seldom can we do something once and be successful. An experience common to many children is learning to ride a bike. Talk about a learning curve! The challenges and fear associated with that process seem insurmountable at first. Motivation and awareness help us to move past our initial fear, especially with the encouragement and support of others. We try, we fail. We try again, we fail again. But each time we learn, and soon we're wobbling along the path to flourishing. This is the value of failure.

The bike analogy illustrates the value of normalizing failure. After a few bruised knees and perhaps a bruised ego, we realize that falling is part of the learning process. It's as if we've signed a contract with ourselves, agreeing to pay a price in bumps and bruises for the joy of riding down a path with our friends. Unless we sign the contract, there will be no such payoff. Failure is built into the learning plan and we accept that as a condition.

The contract can contain sub-clauses. Once we've mastered the basics—starting, steering, and stopping on demand—we make additional deals. If we want to perform skid stops, jumps, and wheelies, we must strike a new bargain, exchanging additional failure for greater rewards. The path from fear to flourishing passes through failure. We can detour around it on foot or we can speed through it on a shiny bike.

Think of three accomplishments in your life: perhaps learning to ride a bike, passing your driver's test, and graduating from high school. Did you make any mistakes when you were learning? How long and hard was it for you to get through these three common life milestones? Most of us have had some level of challenge in one or more of these. What keeps us going is having a clear vision and commitment to keep trying until we're successful.

## Turn Your Life into a Movie You'd Watch Over and Over

Think of one failure you've encountered in your life in which you persevered and ended up feeling proud of your accomplishment. As you reflect on this experience, imagine that you're playing a movie of these events in your mind. The opening scene is where you move from *fear* of trying through *failure*. The drama builds as you *focus* on establishing the foundation you need to be successful. The climax—the do-or-die point—comes when you start to see the results of your efforts, when you *finish*. Finally, the happy ending arrives with the realization that you're now *flourishing*. It's a satisfying movie —a feel-good movie—and it deserves to be rerun often.

As your mental projector recreates the images, pause to take note of each scene and the different emotions attached to it. As you reflect on this success story, consider what drivers helped you to be successful by asking yourself two simple questions:

Why did I succeed?

What moved me through failure?

It's important to celebrate success. When you pause to look at your life and identify the good things, the results can be life-changing. You realize that you can be the main scriptwriter of your life story; you can change your leading role, revise your future, even help write your ending. Whether you see your role as actor, scriptwriter, or director, the focus is up to you.

The *positive principle*[7] suggests that to achieve personal growth, it's helpful to focus on your strengths first. When you look at your successes, you can always find positives; when you replay your failures, you must ensure that you look through the proper lens.

What are your strengths?

_____

_____

_____

## Manage Irrational Thinking

Two single people make eye contact across a crowded room, yet neither makes a move. Why don't they get up and introduce themselves? A well-qualified candidate doesn't apply for a much-desired job. Why do they hold themselves back? After years of clinical work, I believe the reason is due to irrational thinking, something along the lines of "I'm not good enough for this person or organization." They believe they'll fail, so they don't try.

Albert Ellis, often called the father of modern-day cognitive-behavioural psychology, asserted that irrational beliefs can be observed in several patterns of thinking. Here are some examples of common, negative belief patterns that can influence thinking:

- Low frustration tolerance—you believe that you can no longer cope with a situation and get upset (e.g., child crying)

- Self-criticism—a belief system that turns inward and attacks (e.g., blaming yourself for everything that goes wrong)

- Over-generalizing—global beliefs (e.g., everybody is angry)

- All-or-nothing thinking—defining the world in clear extremes (e.g., a peer doesn't say hello, so you assume they no longer like you)

- Self-labelling—a label you put on yourself (e.g., stupid)

When you're not aware of them, you can invariably make irrational assumptions without any evidence or facts. A major downside of irrational thinking is that, if left alone, these beliefs become the primary filter that influences how you interpret the world. Consequently, many people end up alone, because that's what their brain told them they would be. It's a self-fulfilling prophecy.

The best failing takes place when you're *doing*. Fake failing happens when you think you'll fail before you even attempt something. I'd rather that people learn to fail through doing. Fake failure is unproductive and harmful. When you are meeting new people, practise clearing your mental screen of judgment and bias—of yourself or of the other person. Consider that most of us just want to get along, be accepted, and meet kind people. Focus on the process of greeting people rather than worrying about what they may think of you.

Until you try, you'll never know. Embracing failure is one way of giving yourself permission to expand and grow. Perhaps meeting a new person is like flipping a coin: there's a fifty-fifty chance they'll want to get to know you. Any Las Vegas bookie would take those odds in a heartbeat.

## Go Easy on Yourself

If failure is holding you back, remember to normalize it and not judge yourself too harshly. You'll benefit from learning and practising self-compassion, which is choosing to treat yourself with kindness and understanding when faced with failure.[8] It's easy to be judgmental, but it's healthier to be kind—to yourself as well as to others. Acknowledge that you're attempting to achieve your goal of moving ahead, and realize that there's no perfection and no learning without some failure.

There is zero chance that you will go through life without any failure. That would presume the possibility of human perfection. Even if you define perfection in the narrowest and shallowest terms, the standard is unattainable. For some, a perfect life means a life of wealth; the more money they have, the closer they are to perfection. But people with money still fail in other areas. The tabloids are filled with stories of celebrities whose lives are miserable.

On the path to learning how to be happy, we often end up going through some failure to achieve a state of happiness. Even then, we continue to face adversity. Challenges must still be overcome because life isn't static. That's why it's helpful to focus on each day as it comes; once it goes by, you never get it back.

## Explore the Facets of Failure

To move through failure, first explore its detours and dead ends. I divide the various types of failure into two broad categories: subjective and objective.

**Subjective failure:** This type of failure is often the hardest to deal with, because it seems to have no redeeming value. In subjective failure, we resist the notion that any learning is taking place as a result of failing. We look at it as more of a binary outcome—succeed or fail—without nuance or mitigating benefit, and we neglect to consider the role that failure can play in our future happiness. We overlook the implications of rejecting failure as a viable option, and we forget that it's also an opportunity that informs us and allows us to be more proactive in the future.

Subjective failure can seem irrational to onlookers. Let's say that you earned a grade of 82 percent on a school test. Not bad, but your expectation had been to score 90 percent. That energy spent on being upset is wasted—it's only a failure in your eyes. For your classmate who got 65 percent, it would have been a phenomenal success. Accept that 82 percent is a good mark and that there's also room for improvement. It's more empowering to focus your energy on learning and finding opportunities for improvement than to engage in counterproductive self-criticism because you've failed to reach a self-imposed goal.

**Objective failure:** This type of failure may be easier to accept, depending on who experiences it and the value they attach to the loss. It differs from subjective failure in one key respect: before you start a task, you know there's a chance that you'll fail, but you're willing to take the risk. That doesn't mean that you *believe* you'll fail. Objective failure is knowing that while there could be pain, the benefits of success are greater, so you can be motivated and allow yourself to take a chance to achieve a new outcome.

Think of your favourite pro athlete or pop singer. When they perform in front of an audience, they're expected to nail it every time. Of course, athletes have off days and singers sometimes miss their notes. But despite knowing there's a risk of failure, they give it their all every time. Their expectations remain sky-high, and failure never loses its sting. But they have learned to deal with such situations; they have a plan to get back on track.

If someone is trying to eat healthily and exercise consistently for ten days, then they slip on day eleven, they shouldn't focus on that one bad day. Instead, they should put things into perspective and consider that it's just one day out of eleven. The opportunity to build on prior success resumes on day twelve. Anticipating occasional setbacks permits us to deal with them. Failing to anticipate setbacks can prove overwhelming—even defeating. When we're trying to advance, we must be willing to strike a bargain, knowing that subjective and objective failure are the price to be paid.

If you want to overcome fear and accept the risk of failure, it's important to be crystal-clear on the benefits. Look back at your results in chapter three, when you selected a level and block to work on. Why do you really want to shift your position in the $F$-it model toward flourishing?

Armed with this awareness, the decision to move forward is yours and yours alone. As you think about what the future will look like once you've moved from failing toward achieving your goal, keep in mind that your success will depend on owning your behaviour and the consequences of your decisions. If you commit to not blaming others, agree to seek support, and remain open to ideas and coaching, you will have made significant strides in attaining your goal. It's all about accepting accountability for both success and failure.

## Normalize Grief as Part of Failure

After twenty-eight years of marriage, Ingrid was faced with an impending divorce, something she hadn't planned on. Who plans for divorce almost thirty years in? Feeling shame and guilt, she made an appointment to see me. Before she could deal with her failure, though, she needed to deal with her fear of dying alone. Once we processed this fear, we were able to examine her feelings of failure and her grieving of the loss of one of her most important relationships. A divorce can be as painful to deal with as the death of a loved one.

What helped Ingrid to move forward was to normalize her feelings—she accepted that it takes two people to get divorced, just as it takes two to get married. She realized that her marriage gave her many positive memories, and that she hadn't wasted twenty-eight years of her life. She was able to accept that life is filled with challenges and moving forward requires adapting, changing plans, and taking steps to focus on what's next. Ingrid determined that she didn't have to pressure herself to get into another relationship; she realized that if she committed to herself, she would not be alone. Her action plan included engaging with her adult children more frequently so she could see them and spend time with her grandchildren, volunteering at her church, spending more time with her friends, and taking a few university courses, as she loved learning. (How does that compare to the action plan you created for yourself at the end of chapter four?)

When you experience a loss that consumes your physical and emotional resources, grief is a normal part of the healing process. Grief can create internal storms of emotion and, if acknowledged, will often run its own course. The least effective choice you can make when grieving is to deny your feelings or try to avoid them. To grieve is to allow yourself to embrace, feel, and accept your emotions for what they are. When you allow yourself to experience grief without trying to mask it with alcohol or drugs, tremendous learning and personal gains can result.

Ignorance about grief and its useful role can make it even more frightening, something to be avoided. Perhaps this is why some people don't go after their dreams. They fear failure and the emotions that come with it.

Failure is part of the learning process, and not all failure results in grieving. The impact of failure depends largely on initial expectations and context. We have two basic options when we fail: permanent failure and informed failure.

*Permanent failure* is the belief that once we fail there's no use trying again, because the outcome will always be the same. This negative mindset keeps us from trying and reaching our full potential, thus hampering the learning process. We don't bother looking for role models or teachers, or for new ways to develop the same skill. Instead, we quit and never try again.

*Informed failure* is accepting the notion that we may not yet have all the information and skills we need to be successful. But we can process what we've learned from the experience and try again when we're ready. Informed failure promotes the concept that with failure comes learning. Part of that learning is analyzing what went wrong and why. Once we acquire that information, we can move ahead with renewed energy and a willingness to explore new paths to success. And sometimes external support is part of the picture.

My parents inherently understood this type of failure. When I failed grade two, they didn't just say to try again next year. They thought about the factors that may have led to that outcome. They became proactive, removing some of those negative factors and adding new ones that would be helpful. They ensured that I would have a different teacher and sent me to a one-hour reading class at the end of each day to improve my chances of succeeding.

## Internal and External Support

When facing failure, we have two strong support systems to call on. We can look inward for answers and draw on our experience, as well as on our heart and intellect. We can also look to the outside and find role models. Both internal and external sources have much to offer, and a combination of the two can be formidable.

Anyone who has tried to learn a musical instrument or a craft like woodworking knows that it takes time to develop a skill, and that failure is part of the process. To move past failure, you have to intentionally apply yourself to the task.

Psychologist Albert Bandura taught that you can master a skill in four ways:[9]

- Attention—observing the desired behaviour in others who have successfully mastered the skill
- Memory—making notes and studying others so you're clear on what they did and why they did it
- Imitation—practising what you've learned to see if the new knowledge and skills are of value
- Motivation—accepting that you're responsible for motivating yourself to carry out the new actions

Bandura's focus on attention as one way to achieve mastery is a way of accessing external support, including observing those who have succeeded in areas where you have fallen short. If you were a young football player committed to succeed and be a starter, you wouldn't emulate the guy who misses practice and then sits on the bench; you'd model yourself after the player who made the most tackles or caught the most touchdown passes. They're almost always the ones who stay after practice to work on their game. They also tend to be the ones with a positive attitude and who role-model success.

Your mental health can be taxed when you fail. Consider your options for internal and external support if you're struggling to try again. When failure hurts or when you feel stuck, to whom will you talk?

## Failure and Its Impact on Life Satisfaction

The psychology of failure can have a positive or negative impact on your life satisfaction, depending on the lens you're looking through. Each day that you interact with your environment, you receive information that you quickly categorize as positive or negative.

Negative stimuli come in many forms and carry differing levels of significance, ranging from mild (someone took your parking spot), to medium (colleagues dropped the ball on a project), to major (your spouse wants a divorce). These forms are overt: you can see and feel them as they happen.

You can also be influenced covertly by negative influences. These stimuli can shape your behaviour and even impact your health and choices. For example, researchers have found that peer experiences and social norms set by peers can influence eating habits and physical activity.[10]

Most stimuli, whether they are positive or negative, come without much notice through one of your five senses. The senses help process enough of the information to enable you to determine if a stimulus is good or bad.

To move past failure, it can help to understand what impact positive and negative stimuli can have on your overall perception of life satisfaction. If it's true that perception can become reality, it's important to decide what failure means to you, what it is and what it isn't, and what it looks like. Such insights dictate your response and influence your thoughts, decisions, and behaviours. Therefore, your perception determines your reaction and the impact the event has on your overall life satisfaction.

Failure is dynamic, never static. What was easy on one day can be hard on the next. It's important to know up front that you may take two steps forward and one step back, and that success is never a straight line. The goal of the *F*-it model is to tame failure so that you can move through each step and focus on the effort needed to achieve the end goal.

What's the worst thing that can happen if you fail?

_____

_____

When will you know that you're okay with your failure and understand that it's a part of your learning process?

_____

_____

Are you feeling that you're failing because you're not doing? What would help you take action again?

_____

_____

The day I failed grade two, my mother told me, "Bill, we have decided to give you another turn at grade two with a new teacher who will be more fun." To add to the fun, she claimed I would be much better off by doing the grade a second time.

Mom was right; the second time around was more fun, much safer—and a lot of work. This new experience of support and mentoring helped me to discover that there might be some hope that I could learn and that it might be worth trying. I didn't have to rely only on myself and my parents anymore. Now I had an external form of support, too, a teacher who cared. My fear and anxiety were still there, but I wasn't living with nothing but distress every day or the negative judgment I had felt from my first grade two teacher.

I still experienced stress, but it was now a safe environment; my new teacher was much kinder. The stress was more eustress that was motivating me to try and to believe that I didn't have to be fearful of school every day. My teacher and my mother also prepared me to accept that failing would be part of my learning process.

It was hard, though rewarding, and I got through grade two. I was still failing a lot, but I wasn't living in fear each day—and I was more comfortable and committed to trying. I knew that I was going to fail often, but if I kept trying I would one day improve. My mother did an excellent job of keeping things simple, working in small actions, and keeping my focus on the now. As she said, "Get through today and enjoy it. Tomorrow will wait for you."

As I entered grade three, I was still worried that I would never be like the other kids. But it seemed like learning was possible, and I started to see some wins that fuelled confidence in my potential to learn. I was starting to focus.

# 6

# FOCUS

SOME OF US view our past through rose-coloured glasses, and I'm certainly not immune. I'm subject to powerful rushes of nostalgia and a genuine longing for the good old days with family and friends in Prince Edward Island. However, looking back with the perspective that only time can provide, my thirteen-year public school experience brought more pain than pleasure. I did have some moderate success playing sports and a reasonable social network. But from a learning perspective, the bright spots were few and far between.

After failing grade two, I was discouraged and resentful that what appeared easy to others was nearly impossible for me. I lacked the strategies that would have helped me learn to read and write. I also struggled with math and science. I did better in courses like history and geography, where I could memorize what the teacher said; they offered me more control. Luckily, most of my teachers cut me some slack for spelling and grammar mistakes. Nevertheless, it was painful to take courses that demanded reading and interpretation for self-study and problem-solving.

Some positives happened when I passed grade two after repeating the year. Passing the grade made me realize that I could recover from a temporary setback and still succeed. My goal was to do whatever was necessary to reach the next grade. With the benefit of hindsight, I now realize that I was not really learning; I was in full survival mode. Failing once was enough for me; it would take me many years to shake the stigma associated with it.

During my years in public school, I was unaware of what's known as *affect polarization*. Whenever I experienced bad stress, I would respond with negative emotions. This mental state not only decreased my ability to solve problems, but it also fed my fears that I would fail again. Researchers suggest that students in the emotional state I was in at the time tend to view stress only as a negative. This erosion of confidence can create a gap in learning, affecting the ability to cope and to positively rebuff stress. If unaddressed, it can have a negative impact on well-being and put you at greater risk for depression.[1]

Failing grade two left me with a constant fear that I would never be able to learn. The period in which that emotion influenced the way I filtered the world (known as the *emotional refractory period*) lasted until my first year of university. The longer a memory and emotion have a grip on you, the more likely this experience will influence your temperament and personality. Ultimately, your ability to focus and push through fears and past failure will shape your mental health.

I do recall instances in public school when for a few brief moments I had a taste of what it felt like to flourish. At the time, I didn't think of those moments as milestones or building blocks; I thought of them as random rays of sunshine in the grey skies of my school years.

As scattered as they were, those experiences created the hope that if I focused, I could graduate grade twelve, as I finally did. After high school, I decided to leave my home province to play football at Acadia University, located in the beautiful Annapolis Valley of Nova Scotia, along the Bay of Fundy, where the highest tides in the world ebb and flow.

It was a big decision to leave home. My parents had been my support system, and our home, my comfort zone. I knew that university would be difficult for me, but I thought that if I could make the varsity football team, I might be able to succeed as a professional. Clearly, I was naive, regarding not only the physical and psychological requirements of university-level football, but also the cognitive ability to read, write, and study plays.

Somehow, I learned to maintain my focus throughout public school and into that first week at Acadia. I was sure that this would be a crossroads in my life, a point when I'd become clear on the true purpose, power, and meaning of focus. When I arrived on campus, my horizons seemed unlimited, but the clouds of doubt soon moved back in. Within weeks, my world changed. A chain of events pulled me back to a dark place, and I experienced feelings I hadn't had since grade two.

The first link in that chain came when my English professor informed me that my reading and writing skills were below university standards. He suggested that I was most likely performing below a grade eight level. I was told there was no way I would ever be able to graduate university with my skills. However, I decided that I would not drop English. I would keep going and take my chances on getting an F (fail), rather than a W (withdrawn). Despite a lot of frustration and effort on my part, I got an F.

The second link came when I realized that I couldn't learn the football plays. I was used to high school, where the playbook consisted of a few basic calls. If I forgot one, I could ask the player beside me and he would point me in the right direction. As the first few weeks passed, I was having a hard time with almost all of my courses. I was failing at pretty much everything, including football. I felt as if I was in freefall. I was concerned about the amount of money I had spent, and worried about how I would ever pay off my student debt if I didn't get my degree and a good job. Yep, at age nineteen my master plan of pro football fame and fortune was not working out.

And then came a turning point. I shared my academic and athletic concerns with a dear friend and golf buddy from Newfoundland. He listened patiently and, at the end of our conversation, he put a big smile on his face and summed up my predicament in a colourful down-east phrase: "Yep, the arse fell out of 'er for ya." No matter how I looked at my situation, he was right. The arse had indeed fallen out of 'er.

At this juncture, passing was no longer just an option; it was a must. To graduate, I would need to demonstrate academic ability at the standard set by the university. My focus had to change. I had to forget about getting through on good behaviour. I would have to learn the curriculum and demonstrate competency at the university level. This was becoming a major *F*-it moment for me. What could be the harm of trying?

I was lucky that I ended up at a wonderful university. Acadia is one of the top liberal arts universities in Canada; classes were small and teachers' commitment to students was high. I was about to discover a whole new support system and discipline.

Throughout high school, I had become so caught up in passing that I'd neglected to lay the building blocks for learning, most likely because I'd convinced myself that I couldn't do the things others could. I had developed my own ways to get through public school and into university. After repeating grade two, I changed my approach to managing myself each day in school. I was polite, I developed the ability to memorize what my teachers told us, I sat at the front of the class, I didn't engage with or support peers who were goofing off in class, and I was active in school activities and sports. I wasn't much into doing homework, as I found it too hard, so my average was low. I wouldn't get into Acadia today with the grades I had back then.

In my third week of university, a five-minute conversation with a professor changed my life and resulted in my focus shifting from passing to learning. After exchanging a few pleasantries, she asked me how long I had struggled with my learning disabilities. "I've had a hard time learning throughout my entire school life," I told her. She invited me to come back to her office the next day to talk about things the university could do to help.

After some follow-up conversations with her and other officials, she laid out a plan to support and direct me to focus on learning and doing the groundwork needed to learn how to learn. She became a positive mentor and a one-woman support system. She encouraged me and she believed in me. She was exactly what I needed at that low point in my young life. Her words and actions sparked the fire within me, inspiring me to move from my fear of failure and rejection to focusing on those things I could control.

I truly thought I had been trying to learn, but I discovered that I'd merely been trying to pass—to get by. This professor helped me understand that there was nothing wrong with my IQ, that I was more than smart enough for university. My challenge, she said, was adapting; I had to approach learning in a different way. No longer should I permit my ADHD and dyslexia to hold me back from the education and career I wanted.

This professor wasn't just talk. She took a personal interest in me and ensured that I could access the necessary accommodations to my style of learning: things like oral exams, extra test time, and tutors. She also encouraged openness with my professors, and as it turned out, they were all willing to support me. This allowed me to focus on completing courses, not just with a pass, but having acquired actual knowledge. With each course, I started to feel the joy of flourishing and the pride of passing and knowing that I wasn't just checking the box, I was mastering the art of learning.

## Focus Is an Action

When we decide to focus our cognitive and emotional resources on an activity of interest, that focal area becomes the centre of our engagement. Having said that, there are degrees of focus, from low to high. If you're trying to read a book and the TV is on and the phone keeps ringing, there's a high probability that your attention and focus are less than 100 percent.

One of the most pervasive of our modern challenges is *information overload*. Psychologist James Grier Miller first used this term in 1960, when he wrote about information input overload and psychopathology.[2] He listed his concerns about the volume of reading material people had to deal with, and its impact on society generally and on the individual. That his comments were made before the advent of the internet makes them even more relevant in today's high-tech world. Miller was a visionary; early on he identified a concern that now affects everyone. In this era of countless TV networks, multiple computer platforms, and expanding social media possibilities, the art of focus is being lost.

Faced with this onslaught of information, we benefit when we learn to be selective in our focus. Focus requires a commitment. It means allocating time to process the meaning of communications, and in many cases time to craft a response. A difficult email from a customer, peer, or boss can take hours to deal with. While this is going on, the world doesn't stop, and more emails keep coming in.

Most people understand that we can't lessen the amount of information that's arriving. We can only change how we interact with it. For instance, I realized that if I left all my email until the end of the day, I'd have a few hundred messages to deal with. I decided to rethink the way I process them and the weight I put on them. As emails come in, I respond quickly with my intentions for further action, or delete them if I see that I have no action. I figure that if I make the wrong decision and delete an email, the sender can always try again.

I concluded that focusing two hours a day on emails was not time well spent. I use LinkedIn to post my articles, and when I make a posting, I scan for interesting stuff. I use the same approach on Twitter. I don't find it helpful to spend hours on social media; instead, I choose to use the time working with people face to face. It's in our own best interests to customize a personal strategy for dealing with the ever-growing flow of information.

One study published in 2016 addressed Japanese Twitter users suffering from information overload. Despite the volume, users didn't reduce their efforts to gain new followers. They also continued to expand the list of people they would follow.[3] All they changed was their usage habits with respect to reviewing all tweets. They wanted to receive *even more information* because that meant more connections with people, but they accepted that they would not be able to process all the information. So the question is: How much information that's being sent to people is actually useless, since they have no time to process it?

The implications of such information overload on our focus are obvious. Every day, we're subjected to reams of information that all compete for our attention. It's like trying to focus on a game of chess in a pinball arcade. Everywhere we turn, the internet, email, and social media are trying to attract our notice.

Even when we seek information on the internet, the sheer number of options can be overwhelming and frustrating. An excess of sources can discourage us from looking, because we're no longer sure what we're looking for. There's too much data to review and we waste time going to multiple sites before finding the right one. One study confirmed that individuals seeking health information online stopped trying because they were overloaded by the vast array of options.[4] Companies know that if we don't find what we're after on page one, many of us will give up; that's why they pay so much to be on Google's first page.

One challenge is that people are not slowing down and focusing on learning what they need to solve a life challenge. Perhaps that's why there seems to be a movement to do things in small chunks, such as microsurveys and micro-learning modules. The belief is that people don't have time to focus or are too busy to slow down and ponder. While micro-behaviours are important for making change over time, these micromodels suggest that learning and self-discovery need to be done in units of under ten minutes. I've observed that some employers believe that the solution is to assign work in small units of time, without noticing that three small units can psychologically feel like more work than one larger one.

Microlearning can be helpful in the right context. Your experience ultimately defines what's good and bad. If you're learning in small doses, you need to be aware of your overall learning progress and purpose; likewise, if you're making small behaviour changes, you need to chart progress over time and work toward a larger purpose.

## How Purpose Strengthens Focus

Many of us are just trying to keep our heads above water. We must get to work, get through the day, return home, do chores, support our community, nurture our family, check in with friends, eat healthily, allow time for a workout, and get a good night's sleep. Sound familiar? And how much of the noise in your head is less about doing and achieving, and more about fear and failure?

Purposeful focus is stepping off the treadmill of life with the conscious intention to invest mental energy and time in obtaining a desired outcome. Only when you can manage competing demands from your environment can you find the mental space to focus on what you want to accomplish.

When you woke up this morning, what was the single most important thing you wanted to accomplish during the day? This question feels a bit heavy; it might even sound like an existential probe into the meaning you seek for your life. Relax, it's not that complicated. The purpose of the question is simply to help you to discover the degree of purpose or engagement in what you most care about achieving today. The highest level of purpose will inevitably receive the most energy and focus. Why? Because you care about it.

Many people don't wake up with a defined purpose; they awake to a list of things they think they need to do. A defined purpose sets priority so that you can decide what in your life is important, and filter out what's not.

So, what's the most important thing you want to accomplish today? How does that relate (or not) to your level and building block? Do you need to shift your priority?

_____

_____

After my first month at Acadia, my world changed. My focus areas were clear: football, classes, and extra help studying to learn. That was my life; I wasn't much of a party person in my first three years. I went out with friends for the odd event, but most Friday nights I was at the library. I didn't have a girlfriend until my fifth year—and that likely wouldn't have happened if she hadn't asked me out.

Focusing on how to learn was the big boulder that I pushed uphill each day. Perhaps my ADHD was a blessing, as I was hyperfocused on achieving the goal of learning. Though it was incredibly hard to stay focused, the pain of failing was often enough to keep me on track and committed to trying each day to figure out how to learn.

For me, life is about choices. When it comes to focus, there are short- and long-term benefits. Eating a pizza and drinking six beers is a short-term focus. Of course, the long-term impact of repeating this behaviour can prove damaging to our health. To create the success you want, your focus must be clear on what you want and why.

Having a purposeful focus doesn't condemn you to a life of privation. The wonderful thing about focus is that it creates action. Having clarity on what success is and the benefits that come with it provide the foundation for achieving your goals. In addition, when you really focus on something, you're more likely to enjoy the process and commit to working hard and pushing yourself with a smile instead of a frown.

When you have a defined purpose, you can understand not only why what you're doing is important, but also how to be accountable for your actions to achieve that purpose. If you start your day without a defined purpose, you're vulnerable. You can easily become distracted by the many demands for your time. You're like a weathervane, directing your efforts in whatever direction the wind blows. You're subject to the whims of your environment, spreading your focus from one task to another. You expend your energy trying to keep up to what you believe is important, based on the random information placed in front of you.

The risk of living in this state is that it can easily become ingrained. If the daily routine continues, you switch to auto-pilot. Your life and sense of happiness become shaped and influenced by external events. If they're good, you're likely feeling okay. If not, you feel lost and worried. The big risk with not having a daily purpose is uncertainty. Eventually, you can start to question why you get up and do what you do every day. The longer this continues, the emptier you feel. A perceived loss of control and frustration follow.

Purpose can even influence lifestyle habits—those behaviours that become ingrained and turn on automatically in conditional context. Habits form because focus provides an opportunity for repetition and practice until the behaviour becomes part of our behavioural system.[5] Habit formation doesn't occur without such focus. Researchers have postulated that our sense of intrinsic reward and our feelings of accomplishment can help us move from focused behaviour to positive habits.[6]

Being focused on a worthwhile goal feeds your sense of purpose and provides motivation to complete a task. This sense of purpose in one area has a spillover effect: it can provide the drive to keep you moving through life.[7]

Life is constantly changing. The days of creating a single, comprehensive plan for a thirty-year span are gone. Technology will continue to advance at a dizzying pace. Rather than isolating yourself from the resulting societal changes, you need to be open and responsive to them and keep pace with this brave new world.

The first step is to decide on an area of focus. Think back to chapter three, when you selected a level of your life pillar and a building block in that level that needs attention. Focus is key to moving through the *F*-it process—you can determine where your energies are best spent, and which focus will give you the most benefit over the shortest period. After all, life is still happening all around you, and your other commitments don't take vacations.

It's to your advantage to be clear on the purpose and value of your specific focus area. This can enhance self-regulation skills and increase your likelihood of remaining riveted on the target and not falling victim to procrastination and other negative influences.[8]

Psychologists Carol Ryff and Corey Keyes define purpose as a main factor for predicting a person's likelihood of experiencing a positive sense of well-being.[9] This mental clarity boosts a person's sense of purpose and allows them to evaluate their decisions and intentions. One line of research suggests that there's a direct relationship between purpose and life span in adults. People who have a defined purpose and wake up each day with a focus and reason for getting out of bed live longer and happier lives than those who fail to find their purpose.[10]

Purpose creates the mental state and intention to accomplish, evolve, learn, grow, and develop. It motivates us to start, and enables us to finish. Purpose keeps us in the present moment, developing and learning in the now. Thinking about what could be is useful, but not unless actions are taken to make those dreams come true. An absence of purpose may be one reason why some people struggle to flourish.

When you're committed and dialled in to what you're doing, your attention is more likely to become occupied by the task at hand than paralyzed by fear or failure. You're less inclined to procrastinate and more motivated to finish what you start. A deep sense of purpose sparks excitement and offers intrinsic rewards, which feeds your commitment to staying on task. Thinking is wonderful, as it can prepare the game plan for success. But only by *doing* do we move forward in life.

All those nights when I was sitting at the library studying and my friends were out having fun, what kept me going was the feeling of pride and accomplishment from spending four productive hours improving my learning skills. I knew that each hour took me one step further down the path to learning how to flourish. However, to take this step, I needed a structured plan for how I would learn. The university provided accommodations, such as doing tests orally until my writing skills improved. A tutor who specialized in dyslexia helped me develop learning strategies. I committed to learning as my number one priority, which can be hard in a university setting where there are so many opportunities to choose fun.

Researchers have found that workers can create pride in their jobs by overcoming barriers and creating the sense of well-being that comes from doing.[11] Ford Motor Company had a slogan that "Quality is Job #1." A worthy goal indeed, and one that requires maximum effort. My job was learning, and I'm convinced that my intense focus helped me develop a sense of pride in myself. My focus on accomplishment was like a miracle drug; it had a profound impact on my overall mental well-being. By doing, I was much closer to finishing and flourishing than to fear or failure.

The clearer you are on the purpose of your focus, the more motivated you'll be to do the work, seek support, and focus. Focusing with intention on something you want is a fuel that drives your behaviours to achieve a desired outcome. Failure and its associated risk of fear can impair your ability to focus. When you experience these moments of fear, focusing on the process instead of the outcome can direct you again.

> "When you are working on something, and you're working well, you have the feeling that there's no other way of saying what you're saying."

MIHALY CSIKSZENTMIHALYI

## Enter the Zone

The more you practise with purpose, the more you increase your ability to experience flow. Anyone who's focused and committed to learning and mastering a skill is positioning themselves to "get in the zone." This level of performance isn't just for pro athletes; it's there for anyone who focuses on the everyday tasks they want to master. The concept called *flow*, or being in the zone, can be complex to define, as it has different components. When a person enters flow, their sense of time is distorted, and they lose awareness of and attention to things in their environment.[12]

Naturally, your ability to focus is dependent on your skill level and the challenge you're attempting to overcome. You can enter the zone only when there's a balance between your skill set and the appropriate challenge. You must be engaged, so you don't get bored. The challenge also shouldn't be so high that you run the risk of becoming worried and anxious.[13]

When you enter your zone of focus, you can find your groove—that ideal place where your mental state allows you to perform to your fullest potential. To enter this place, you must have a desire to learn and to master the area of focus. Once there, you become so absorbed in the task at hand that nothing else is of interest or concern. When maintaining focus becomes a positive experience and you're fully in the zone, hours can pass like seconds.

## Choose to Stay Focused

Focus assumes you have a sense of control and believe you can do what you want. Unfortunately, most people, without realizing it, believe in what's referred to as an *external locus of control (ELOC)*. They believe that they have no choice in their behaviour, and that they're essentially reacting to their external world. ELOC is based on a deterministic model that control is out of the individual's hands, and if they're ever to regain control, force and fear will be needed.

Those who have a defined purpose are more likely to live their lives from an *internal locus of control (ILOC)*. They believe that they're in control of their own thoughts, behaviours, and actions, that they have the capacity to choose their own behaviour, and the external world can't be held accountable. In short, when we operate from an ILOC, we understand that we, and not our environment, define what we do and who we are.

Consider your level and building block. Can you attribute what's holding you back to an *internal* locus of control or to an *external* locus of control? If it's external, how can you shift the cause to something within your control?

_____

_____

## Set Clear Goals

To stay focused on something important, you need an achievable but worthwhile goal. A goal provides clarity, direction, motivation, and the impetus for change. Goals can be long term or short term, meaning that you have different expectations as to when you might achieve them. Short-term goals are usually the intermediate steps toward achieving a long-term goal. They're the more tangible and accessible steps that must be completed before reaching the long-term goal. An example of a long-term goal would be creating a vision at age twenty-five of retiring at fifty-five. The short-term goals to achieve this long-term goal may include meeting the maximum retirement contributions each month and researching investment options.

Smaller tasks completed en route provide feedback and motivation along the way, the equivalent of being handed a cup of water partway through a marathon. These periodic achievements serve as milestones that you can celebrate and relish. When you don't set clear goals, those small victories mean little. You're then in danger of slipping from focus back to failure.

Try setting a short-term goal to help you with your level and building block. One model you can use to help set a goal is the acronym SAMPLE:

Specific
Attainable
Measurable
Purposeful
Legal
Ethical

Write down that short-term goal:

---

Setting goals helps you get from point $A$ to point $B$. One metaphor that illustrates why goals are important can be shown using a protractor. If you draw a straight line out from a 90-degree angle ($A$) and extend it to a point representing a distance of five miles ($B$: your goal), you can envision moving from point $A$ to point $B$. Now imagine moving another five-mile line originating from point $A$, but two degrees beyond the first. After five miles you end up at $C$, a significant distance from your goal. You can see how even a small deviation—or gap—in your ability to focus will result in missing your goal. Constantly measuring progress—such as using a daily journal or app to track what you're doing and get ongoing feedback—allows you to make adjustments if you go off course. As well, feedback gives you a sense of accomplishment and shows the rewards for maintaining focus.

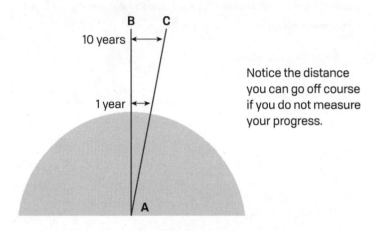

Notice the distance you can go off course if you do not measure your progress.

GOAL SETTING

Another benefit of setting clearly defined goals is that they create a framework for focus and practice. If success is a journey, you must develop your knowledge and skills before you set out on that journey. Finishing the trip takes patience, practice, and a positive attitude. Keep in mind that finishing a goal can often be just the beginning, and you will need to repeat what you did so you can maintain your success. In the next chapter, we'll look more at the power of microgoals to help you finish what you start.

As you set your personal focus goal, it's important to clearly define the time you need to set aside to meet it. In addition, it helps to know the kinds of support you will need to be successful (people, equipment, etc.).

How long will it take to see success?

What supports will you need in place?

To get the most out of life, you must know how best to spend your finite allotment of time. The return on your time investment will depend on your values. You need to ensure that what you focus on and want to achieve is within your control.

On a scale of 1 (low) to 10 (high), how motivated are you to focus on the level and building block you picked?

Anything less than 8 may suggest that you're not ready to make the effort required to reach the finish line. How can you move your focus to 8+?

How will you manage distractions? Locking in a priority can help keep you focused and not distracted by every little stimulus.

---

When you start to focus on goals, you can get stuck and not be sure you know what you can do or how you can do it. You can become distracted. But curiosity can spark interest to help you focus on one area of life you want to master. Curiosity can be defined as the desire to learn something that's perceived to be of value. The more you become engaged in what you're learning, the more likely that the creative part of your brain is open to further exploration that will help fuel your focus. As technology changes and you evolve with it, continuously asking *why* satisfies your curiosity and feeds your creativity.

Researchers have found curiosity to be an essential element in motivating us to act and learn.[14] In addition, curiosity plays an important role in shaping decisions. It influences what you find meaningful and what your focal point will be. Ultimately, curiosity helps determine life direction and choices.[15] Being curious enough about something to focus on it increases your chances of finishing it.

# 7

# FINISHING

O N A WARM June evening on Prince Edward Island, I was
wearing a blue robe and a square-shaped hat with a tas-
sel. As I stood in line with a few hundred of my peers, it
was difficult to shake the feeling that I was an imposter.
A symphony of sound added to my discomfort. Periodic bursts
of applause were punctuated by scraping chairs, dry coughs,
and nervous laughter. Indistinct voices droned from the stage,
distorted by the acoustics of the cavernous hockey arena. I
began to fidget and sweat, distracted by the commotion, but
my emotions remained oddly flat.

As their names were called, students moved quickly
across the stage. They robotically shook the principal's hand,
accepted their diplomas and a few mumbled words of congratulations, and returned to their seats. It all had a strange
assembly-line feel to it. They entered stage left as students

and exited stage right as graduates. I was contemplating what this day meant to me and how this short walk across the stage would change my life.

It had taken me thirteen years to get here—one more than most—and much of it had felt like I was serving time. Graduating public school was supposed to be a big moment, but the feelings of joy and pride I had expected were nowhere to be found. The smile on my face was fake, to hide my inner turmoil. I had focused on this goal every single school day. In fact, because of my dyslexia and ADHD, I had worked harder than most of my peers for the opportunity to savour this moment.

So why was I not feeling the pride, or at least a deep sense of accomplishment? I had built up this day and now that it was here, it felt anticlimactic and bogus. Why didn't I feel the same rush of emotion that I felt after a football win?

Instead of joy, sinister emotions began to take over. As I drew closer to the front of the line, negative thoughts were running through my mind: "You're fooling people and they'll catch you." The accusation came from within; the voice was my own. I had passed fair and square, but inside I felt like an actor playing the role of a high school graduate. It didn't feel real. The final scene of the play was me getting my diploma.

The desire to learn had been such a driving force for me, but now that I was graduating, I was telling myself that I didn't really deserve this diploma. In truth, I hadn't learned that much; my biggest accomplishment was coping and learning how to learn. It's difficult to enjoy a personal accomplishment when you doubt its validity.

My mom and dad were beaming. I was happy I hadn't let them down, even though my marks were low; my overall average was just a bit above 60. I suspected that in some courses I was given a passing mark of 51 because I was a good kid who didn't add to the teachers' stress. They knew I was trying, and I suspect that most of my marks were participation-driven.

I was emotionally confused, unable to process the significance of my accomplishment. I wouldn't—or couldn't—allow myself to celebrate the attainment of this longstanding goal. I truly believed that if you couldn't learn by the time you left high school, you probably never would. What should have been a milestone felt more like a millstone around my neck.

We benefit personally only when we know what success looks like. Only then can we recognize it when it comes; only then can we pause, take a bow, and celebrate our accomplishments.

Unaware that this was just the first leg of my learning marathon, I was unable to appreciate its relevance and the opportunity that awaited me when I took the next big step and entered Acadia University in the fall. When we're unclear on the purpose for reaching a personal milestone, we miss the pride and significance of doing so. In my ignorance, I had attached a different meaning to the feat. When we're under stress, our personal map of the world and our life view can be defined by an isolated moment. Only when we can step back and look at the entire picture are we able to see it objectively.

Finishing something you've focused on is, indeed, evidence of success. However, success can come in many forms. Sometimes it springs from necessity, the fact that you must succeed if you're to avoid negative consequences. At the other extreme, success can become a life-defining moment that brings long-lasting value and joy. Each of our successes falls somewhere on this continuum, from basic survival needs to transformational moments.

Many employees focus on work with the practical mindset of surviving their forty-hour week. At the end of the week there's no intrinsic reward, no sense of pride and accomplishment in their work. The only reward is finishing their five eight-hour days while meeting the minimum requirements of the job. If they maintain that acceptable level, they'll continue to get paid; if not, they'll be fired. Working day after day just to pay the bills can be disheartening. You're living on a continuous loop. You're merely surviving.

I now know that life is a series of milestones, not a race toward a single finish line that requires no further action or focus. On graduation night, I lacked that valuable insight, and I suspect it's what caused my confusion. I had thought that graduating would make life easier because I would have finished learning the things I needed to pursue a career. I was putting unnecessary pressure on myself. I didn't need to have my future mapped out at that exact moment. That was an unreasonable expectation on my part.

After years of emotional pain and a daily diet of education that often left a bitter taste of failure, I felt slow-witted and defeated. Throughout those school years I had struggled to manage anxiety and depression, fearful that I might never get through, that my grade two teacher was right and I would amount to nothing more than a good farmhand.

Knowing that my parents were watching, I fought to keep my composure. They had helped me reach this point, and I wanted them to enjoy the moment. I struggled to focus, for their sake. I needed to look happy. Despite it all, I walked across the stage. Clutching my diploma, I was desperate to return to my seat as quickly as possible. My body refused to move the way I asked it to; it was out of synch with my mind. As I look back, I realize my stress response had kicked in and I was somewhere between fight and flight, which is freeze. All the noise, lights, and stimuli were overwhelming. My feelings of guilt intensified. I navigated the final few steps from the stage fearing that I might faint.

Once I was off the stage, I started to return to normal, as if a switch had been turned off. The one person I spotted, in the sea of parents, was my father. Our eyes locked and he patiently waited for me, as he always did.

Dad was a bartender for fifty years and managed the bars where he worked. His favourite was a place called Top of the Park at the Charlottetown racetrack. Dad was a natural leader, a man I always respected. He ruled our house with kindness but also had firm, non-negotiable expectations. One of the biggest of those was expressed in the command: "Do what your mother says." Dad developed his leadership abilities through sports. He was a local legend—captain and best player on a number of sports teams. He never talked about his athletic accomplishments; people in the community told me the stories. He was a big fish in a small pond, a man who fell in love, stayed in his hometown, and dedicated his life to his wife and children.

Dad was a man of few words, but when he spoke, the message was always powerful and relevant. He knew me inside and out, and now I could see the concern on his face. Of course, Dad being Dad, he would wait until we had a quiet moment alone to discuss it with me. My mother suddenly appeared at his side and dominated the conversation with heartfelt expressions of pride and congratulations. Dad and I were quiet, giving her the opportunity to bask in the moment.

When I arrived home a few hours later, Dad was in the living room, reading in his favourite chair. I knew he was going to ask the question I didn't yet have an answer for. Sure enough, he put his book down and began making small talk, asking me about the ceremony, my friends, football, and things like that. Finally, he came to the point. "What's up, Bill? You look like the cat that ate the family's pet bird and is waiting to get caught."

I paused to gather my thoughts. "I really don't know. I feel guilty, like I've fooled everyone." If it were not for what my dad said next, I likely would not have had the courage to go to Acadia to play football in the fall. His quiet wisdom inspired me to keep trying to learn. I can't tell you how convinced I am that our lives are defined by moments such as this. If we're open to listening, these moments can be transformational, and that's what this moment was for me. This short conversation changed my life for the better.

The sentiments he expressed were unforgettable, even if I can't recall his exact words. Dad always spoke using metaphors that he knew would capture my attention. They were almost like biblical parables. Once I had extracted the nuggets of truth and processed them, they had a powerful impact. Dad helped me reframe my accomplishment. No longer was it tainted by feelings of guilt and inadequacy. He helped me see it as a major milestone in resiliency, self-discipline, and coping. He pointed out that many people with knowledge, skills, and motivation still fail to accomplish the life goals they are capable of. I could see in his eyes that for him these life lessons came from personal experience. Dad had always been my hero and the smartest person I knew. He was brilliant and well-read, with amazing math skills. He could have become anything he wanted to. However, when I was a young child, around the age of four, he lost a business. An Esso service station he owned went bankrupt.

My mom once confided in me that this loss hit him hard and had lasting effects. He gave up his dream of attending college, despite having a full scholarship to Boston University. Mom revealed how he struggled with depression after the bankruptcy. This lifted a veil for me. It explained why he spent so many hours alone and why he was not the most outgoing father. He was always there for us when we needed him, but we were expected to do many things for ourselves.

Dad was even there for customers who came to his bar. Over the years, I saw him support many people who had good jobs but may have had drinking problems, even addictions. He was known for serving Coke with no rum to those he felt had consumed enough alcohol. He knew when they'd reached the point where they wouldn't know the difference. He would take their money and put it in an envelope. The next morning, he'd call the man's wife to come get it, so she could buy groceries.

After my conversation with Dad, I started to feel a deep sense of pride. He had asked me what being smart really meant to me. He told me that there were many kinds of intelligence, and he unpacked some for me. This was before I had ever heard of Howard Gardner, professor of education at Harvard University, who proposed that there are eight different types of intelligences: [1]

- linguistic intelligence (word smart)
- logical-mathematical intelligence (number/reasoning smart)
- spatial intelligence (picture smart)
- bodily-kinesthetic intelligence (body smart)
- musical intelligence (music smart)
- interpersonal intelligence (people smart)
- intrapersonal intelligence (self smart)
- naturalist intelligence (nature smart)

Dad taught me that reading and math were just two among many sets of skills. He told me that I was people smart and that I had the knack of convincing and influencing others. And when Dad said something, you listened, because it was rare for him to make a declarative statement. He let me know how proud he was that I hadn't quit on myself or let down my mother's belief in my potential.

He recommended that in life I should not become an umpire who must make decisions about whether a pitch was a ball or a strike; instead, I should be the pitcher and choose how I wanted to throw the ball and where I wanted it to go. He said, "Bill, you wanted to graduate, and you did. That's a strike. What's your next pitch, son?" I said, "To go to Acadia, make the football team, and graduate university." His response was realistic, affirming, and motivational. "Okay, you have some hard work ahead of you. But for the next few days, enjoy what you have accomplished. And then get at it."

I was now able to enjoy the fact that I had my first major life accomplishment under my belt. I wasn't a fake after all. I was a person trying to figure out my life and the importance of each decision and action that I took. My father's words had made me see the bigger picture. My journey toward learning was not over, but I was starting to become aware of how massive my accomplishment really was. What I had done was laudable: while dealing with mental health issues, I had focused on finishing each day.

Your perspective and your ability to adapt and cope with life's challenges determine not just what you're able to finish, but ultimately what you become. Erase the finish line from your thoughts. Happiness and success require repeating and completing a variety of life activities in respect to money, career, relationships, physical health, and mental health. Life is dynamic. Both energy and resiliency are needed to get the most out of it.

Focusing on what you want is only part of the process, albeit an important part. It still takes affirmative action to finish. During my chat with Dad, I had discovered that knowledge, skills, and motivation don't guarantee success. Finishing things you care about also requires resilience and healthy coping skills.

> "Everything is figureoutable."
>
> MARIE FORLEO

## The 3C Model

To reinforce the concept of finishing, I created a model called the 3C Model, which examines the motivation for change and the likelihood that someone will finish the race they start. The 3C Model stands for *predicting behavioural conviction/ competency/coping skills.* If you monitor how you're doing daily in each of the three Cs, you can determine what you need to do to achieve your desired goal.[2]

- **Conviction:** Making a behavioural change requires strong internal motivation and commitment. Only the individual can define their true *why*, because conviction is more than motivation; it's purpose. It shines a light on the risks and rewards of making a behavioural change. The more you understand these realities up front, the better you can tap into your *why* and maintain your conviction.

- **Competency:** To make a behavioural change, you need to have the knowledge and skills required to achieve the desired result. But you also need to understand the progression and time required to apply these skills. You can often develop a new competency by sequencing information and processing it in small chunks. This allows you to learn in the most efficient and effective way, mastering each step as you go. Lasting change seldom takes place as a result of a single event; it's often the result of making small decisions over and over.

- **Coping skills:** The ability to deal with your daily stress load, problem-solving, and managing conflicting priorities can assist you in staying focused and on track to achieve your desired goal. The better your coping skills, the higher the probability that you'll be able to solve problems, make effective decisions, and manage known and unforeseen life challenges. Those skills create the resiliency to adhere to a daily action plan, which helps you achieve your desired behavioural change.

## How to Make the Change Stick

Perhaps one of the biggest challenges is to stop activities that are not good for us and start activities that we know are good for us. *Adherence* is the ability to comply with action plans that keep us in a state of flourishing. In the medical world, adherence is being studied in detail to determine what can be done better to keep a patient compliant with their medical treatment. For example, one study reported that fewer than 50 percent of patients took the medication they were prescribed to treat a medical issue.[3]

One reason why people regularly fail at their goals may be that they don't allow for life stress. Work and home stressors may affect their priorities and impact their decision-making. People with gaps in their coping skills often have adherence issues. Faced with pressures, they struggle to stick to their well-intentioned plans. Under stress, ambition wavers and they lose some of their resolve. In this vulnerable state, it's easy to slip back into old patterns and habits.

In my clinical work as a counsellor, I support people and help them achieve personal life goals. Over the years, I've watched many people succeed and many fail. Based on my experience and research, I've confirmed what my dad told me so long ago—that merely having the skills, knowledge, and motivation doesn't guarantee success in life, nor does it predict that we'll finish what we start. Without adequate coping skills, it can be hard to move ahead.

In my work, I've seen many people fail and not try again. They became stuck, stopped believing in themselves, and were not capable or sufficiently motivated to move through failure, refocus, and get back to work. They didn't understand that when you run a race, you're going to step in potholes. Succeeding requires getting up, dusting yourself off, and trying again. Accept that if you have gaps in your coping skills, you may want to develop and improve them so that you can better problem-solve to reach your goal.

In what areas do you need to improve your coping skills so you can move forward to complete your goal?

_____

_____

## The Power of Microgoals to Improve Coping Skills

To complete a daily task or reach a personal or professional goal, you must follow clearly defined steps. The more you break your goals down into simple steps, or microgoals, the greater the likelihood that you'll achieve success. The 3C Model helps you create microgoals by examining your underlying motivation for achieving a goal.

Let's look at behaviours that can predict motivation by considering the interaction of conviction, competency, and coping skills. Each of the three *C*s influences the likelihood that you'll cross the finish line; taken together they impact focus, finishing, and flourishing. A weakness in any one can result in frustration or relapse, even failure. You may have conviction and the required competency when you start, but good intentions aren't enough. Do you have the coping skills to get you through when the going gets tough and you want to quit? If—or more likely when—you fail, you can focus on the causes, learn from them, and move forward to cross your defined finish line.

Understanding why and how failure happens helps you to anticipate it and head off the destructive emotions and negative self-talk that failure can generate. It's fantastic to have a clear purpose, but it can feel unattainable if it's not grounded in reality and daily actions—and microgoals set your conviction in motion.

You may lack information or skills when you set out to complete a big goal. Your microgoals, then, could consist of gathering this information and strengthening these skills every day. For example, you want to start eating better. First, you'll need to define what "better" looks like. Your microgoals might be reading up on nutrition or consulting a dietitian, incorporating three more fruits and vegetables into your daily meals, and learning how to prepare a stir fry or another healthy dish.

To complete a goal, you must learn to manage the demands and priorities that compete for your time. Faced with this daily menu of challenges and choices, you must problem-solve and make good decisions under pressure. If you can create small, measurable goals each day, you'll be better able to cope when life throws you a curve ball. The challenge with emotions is that there's no off switch. If you don't have the skills to manage and cope with emotions, they can distract you from finishing what you start.

You have to face the fact that you might not complete your big goal overnight. Even with the best intentions, you likely won't be able to run a marathon in two weeks if you've never jogged around the block. Using the 3C Model, determine what microgoals you can set and act on *today* in order to move toward your larger goal; this will hold you accountable for changing your behaviour and boost your resiliency.

## Conviction

I want to change _____

from _____ to _____

because _____

## Competency

The knowledge and skills I must have to be successful are:

_____

It will take me _____

*(amount of time)* to see results.

## Coping skills

If I am faced with a challenge or problem or barrier, I will use the following to cope:

_____

Set your completion date: _____

Be sure to celebrate your success when you achieve your goal!

## Building Your Resiliency Reserve

Resiliency is not a trait, it's a coping skill that you can learn and develop. Resiliency can help you find the energy and focus to push forward and finish what you start, even in the hard times. There will always be more obstacles in your path; it's your choice whether you keep going or stop. How well you develop and refine your resiliency determines how well you will recover from stressful experiences and overcome hardships.[4]

Resiliency gives you the drive to take on the daily demands of life—those potholes and detours that can drain your power reserves. Without sufficient energy to push forward, you can quickly lose hope. And if you lose hope, you're at risk psychologically and more likely to question why you bother to go on.

Resiliency provides the energy to work toward a solution. The higher your resiliency reserves are, the more prepared you are to deal with whatever comes your way. Resiliency levels are like a cellphone battery with a limited charge. If the battery has just 10 percent life remaining and you need to place a long call, you know you need to recharge it. If your resiliency battery is drained when you begin your journey toward change, you risk losing hope and the will to keep going. When it's fully charged, you're less likely to be sidelined by unexpected challenges. As wonderful as life is, it's full of such challenging moments. Resiliency can be a valuable ally as you take on those challenges.

Don't confuse persistence with resiliency. Sometimes we can be too persistent and we don't know when to quit. We continue to battle on, in the face of certain defeat. On the surface, this may sound noble, the stuff of heroism. But it can also be folly that serves only to waste our energy on a hopeless cause. If I dream of being a pro golfer, I may soon become frustrated and drain all my reserves, emotionally and financially, focusing on a goal that's impossible to achieve.

Resiliency is about maintaining a charge and using it to achieve a realistic goal. Flourishing is being able to maintain the charge, which can fuel your resiliency. The process of creating and maintaining energy reserves starts with self-awareness—what builds you up and what draws you down. Resiliency isn't static; it's dynamic and dependent on what you do to build it.

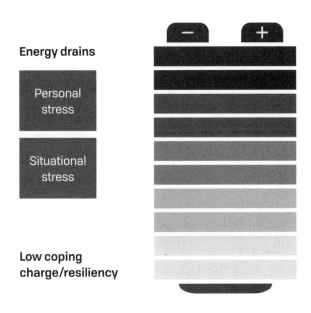

**Energy drains**

Personal stress

Situational stress

**Low coping charge/resiliency**

THE RESILIENCY BATTERY

Your daily life microdecisions and activities determine the kind of charge you add to your resiliency battery. The forces that can drain energy come in different orders of magnitude (low/medium/high), and these forces can vary from day to day. Your resiliency quotient determines how ready you are to take on new demands as they present themselves. Because coping skills interconnect with physical, mental, and life factors, you can exert direct control over them. But to do that, you must first understand them.

Resiliency can be built by the things you do at work and during leisure time. Exercise, healthy relationships, and financial stability all add to the reserve. My dad's eye-opening lesson on what I had accomplished by graduating provided my first foray into the world of resiliency, how it can be developed, and how important it is for success.

## Total Wellness

Looking back, I believe that Dad's talk planted the seeds of an idea that I refer to today as *total wellness*. Based on my own experience and subsequent research, I have determined that the four components of total wellness are physical health, mental health, coping skills, and life skills. Balance is at the core of total wellness.

Our resiliency charge depends on how much we invest in each of the four components of total wellness. Their purpose is to offset the energy drains that we experience. What we eat, how we sleep, our physical activity, our budget and disposable cash, and the time we spend with our children and partners all influence our total wellness and determine our resiliency charge. Life can infuse us with power or drain that power.

We flourish when we develop the confidence to choose what we really want in life. Sure, our struggles can be draining, but if we turn them into opportunities that allow us to flourish, they can also be empowering. Before that can happen, though, we must accept that we alone determine whether our challenges are destructive or mentally invigorating.

Your mental health shapes what you do, and what you do determines your resiliency. However, even if you possess a high resiliency level, some events can be overwhelming. Everyone has a limit. First responders witness trauma every day, but even these hard-nosed professionals are human beings first. They never know when a call may impact them in a way that puts them at risk for post-traumatic stress disorder. As mortals, we're all vulnerable. Sudden shock and grief can bring even the strongest people to their knees. When this happens, it's crucial to remember that this is normal, not a sign of weakness.

If you find yourself repeatedly and regularly unable to cope with life, it's wise to talk to a mental health professional. If you break a leg, the natural and accepted thing to do is to see a medical doctor. Mental health is no different. It's wise to tap into the knowledge base of trained professionals. They can provide insights that most lay people lack and can assist you in getting back on a sound mental footing.

Coping skills can help you overcome challenges and pressures, so you can stay focused on your desired goal. Resiliency is dynamic, and your total wellness plays a role in providing the energy to finish what you start. When coping skills are firmly in place, they support and enhance problem-solving and decision-making. Like learning the ABCs and multiplication tables, these skills become hardwired and we can use them on demand.

*Cognitive hygiene* influences mental health, which in turn affects the behaviours, actions, and choices that impact our resiliency. I define cognitive hygiene as the practice of effectively managing negative thinking while maintaining the ability to problem-solve and make good decisions. Many people are stuck in a "stinking thinking" mode that inhibits these abilities. Much as oral hygiene rids us of harmful bacteria, cognitive hygiene protects us from thinking errors that can influence our mental health. And like oral hygiene, cognitive hygiene is dependent on daily practice and self-examination. Invariably, what we think affects what we do. Creating habits that can keep the mind clear and our thoughts positive helps promote mental health, and thus, total wellness.

As I deconstruct my past and reflect on how I got through grade twelve, I realize that my success was dependent on support systems and coping skills. I learned how to confront my daily fear of failure and maintain my focus on each grade as it came. At the time, I was unaware of the existence of specific coping microskills that can be taught. Once learned, these skills can have a profound and positive impact on your ability to finish what you want to accomplish.

At the end of chapter four, you created an action plan to address your chosen level and building block. Go back now and review it to ensure that you've thought through all the supports and skills you'll need to finish your goal.

Is there anything you want to add or adjust?

---

---

## Less Is More

For a growing number of people, less is more. That philosophy also applies to selecting goals. Taking on and attempting to finish too many tasks serves only to dilute your stores of energy. As a result, nothing gets done. Choose your goals with care, and realize that finishing them requires total commitment. When you fail to honour your commitments, the result can be discouraging, even devastating. Trying and failing is one thing, but failing through lack of effort is quite another. Before you commit, assess the practicality of the goal, establish a reasonable timeline for meeting it, and be aware of all the conflicting interests that will compete for your energy and focus.

It's helpful to set realistic expectations, but be mindful not to limit your dreams. Allow yourself to dream big. When you start something that you want to accomplish, be clear on the milestones, driven by microgoals, so that you can use them as checkpoints to ensure you're going in the right direction. Finishing each milestone is an accomplishment, and these milestones can also give you affirmation that you're one step closer to achieving your larger goal—a sense of accomplishment can re-energize you, propel you forward, and allow you to measure your progress. Please treat yourself with compassion when you try, but fail, to achieve the desired outcome. Remember: unless you try, you can't succeed.

The more you can focus on the process rather than the outcome, the better you'll be able to manage your physical, cognitive, and emotional resources. Once you demonstrate that you can achieve something, you're in a position to replicate it, which in turn positions you to experience the benefits of flourishing.

# 8

# FLOURISHING

BOUGHT MY FIRST home in 1990—a major milestone—three years after graduating university. Back then, a young graduate could still enter the housing market. This home represented the *F*-it model in action: I had learned how to finish in my financial level, putting money away each month into my savings, and had accumulated my down payment.

Now that I owned my first shelter, I also had my first mortgage to pay, and I quickly learned about the many other expenses attached to home ownership. My wife, Sherrie, and I barely had enough money to cover the monthly bills. Sherrie devised an amazing budget that we followed exactly—no exceptions. We had to be focused and follow our plan each month to stay on track and on budget.

Those were great years; we had everything that we really needed. But we still met with a financial planner to see where we could improve. Once the planner analyzed our cash flow and how we spent our money, she chuckled. She informed us that there was little she could do until we added to our monthly income, as our budget accounted for almost every dollar we spent. Once our bills were paid, we had a grand total of $268 remaining at the end of the year.

Because we kept such tight control of the purse strings, we felt we were starting to flourish financially. We had what we wanted, and even had enough money to give to the church, support a child in a developing country through the Foster Parents Plan, and care for our two cats. All those years of focus and finishing one thing at a time were starting to pay off. The sense of pride in being able to support a foster child in Africa was a major milestone for this adopted adult.

For the first time, I started to feel that I was flourishing in my learning, as well. Graduating Acadia University with a BSc in physical education and BA in teaching gave me the assurance that I would be more—and accomplish more—than some people had thought, and it put me on the path to gainful employment and financial independence.

With my undergraduate degree in hand, I completed my teaching practicum and was licensed to teach in the province of Nova Scotia. I was also employed as a youth worker, supporting young offenders who were experiencing mental health and addictions issues. I'd always wanted to help people. As early as elementary school, I felt good inside when I did things to support others.

I was on my own as a responsible adult taxpayer, contributing to my community. I had my own income, and I owned every decision I made—good or bad. I was gaining confidence that I could not only learn but excel in my learnings, that I could do something that held meaning for me.

Two years after I started my job and bought the house, I knew it was time to return to university and work toward my master's in counselling psychology. I thought that if I could achieve that level of education, it would be enough.

Sherrie had bought a Gold Crown Hallmark store and was building a business in our community. I was in graduate school, working full time, and coaching university football. Life was busy and rewarding. We had a structured daily routine that was perfect for my ADHD brain. By any measure, I was flourishing.

When you have clear evidence that you're finishing what you started, you position yourself to flourish. *Flourishing* is defined as maintaining a desired outcome through engaging in a set of daily habits or behaviours.[1] For the purposes of this book, flourishing means that you've brought one of your five levels and all the building blocks within it to a condition where you feel you're working toward ensuring the mental health you desire. The more levels you get to this state, the better your mental health is. When you're flourishing in one or more levels, you're functioning at your best almost all the time—like an engine firing on all cylinders. You feel in harmony and balance.

Addressing and improving your mental health is at the core of the *F*-it process of achieving a desired outcome. No matter the level or building block, when you're interested in moving from fear to flourishing, you benefit by being clear on the value to yourself and the people you care most about.

The term *value* refers to a fundamental belief of what is most important to us. Our values help us make our decisions with respect to what we believe is right or wrong, or what is good or bad for us. Common core values a person may choose to live their life by include family, health, kindness, honesty, integrity, love, and creativity. You must first define these core values as being critical and important. When they are, these characteristics motivate and guide your decision-making.

While the previous four chapters have moved you along in the *F*-it process, this chapter's goal is to provide some insights that can help you keep flourishing once you've arrived.

The goal of resiliency is to build reserves and capacity to push through life's challenges. Those reserves are then available when you're taxed. Resiliency depends on what you do daily to maintain your physical, mental, work, relationship, and financial health.

Flourishing creates the motivation and energy to tackle those things that you're passionate about. It can motivate you to not just maintain what you have, but also to evolve and grow. If resiliency is about charging your batteries, flourishing is like creating your own battery charger to fuel your resiliency.

## Flourishing Contributes to Happiness

If we get to the point where we're flourishing in each or most of the five levels, we're likely in the right frame of mind to engage in prosocial behaviours such as volunteering and performing acts of kindness for others,[2] which can boost our happiness[3] and help us live out our values. When we're flourishing, we feel positive about what we're doing for ourselves and others. It's a state of optimal mental health that includes self-acceptance (or more technically, positive psychological functioning).[4] This isn't good only for ourselves, but it's also good for all those around us. We're more likely to want to do things to help others.[5] Researchers have found that performing acts of kindness enriches both the giver and the receiver. The benefits to the receiver are obvious. The giver gets additional opportunities to experience positive emotions like love and trust.[6] And we're less likely to miss work or let family members down by not following through on commitments.[7]

Flourishing typically includes positive emotional well-being (positive emotions and thoughts around life satisfaction), positive psychological functioning (self-acceptance, personal growth, autonomy, positive relations with others), and positive social functioning (social acceptance, social support, and integration).[8] In short, feeling happy about life.

Two models that help us understand happiness are *hedonic well-being* (experiencing pleasure) and *eudaimonic well-being* (fulfilling our purpose in life).[9] Aristotle considered eudaimonia to be the highest good for self and others,[10] meaning flourishing is not just about ourselves; it's about what we can do to support the people in our lives.

As difficult as it was for me, the learning process put me on the right path and helped me identify my life purpose. I realized that my hard-won education equipped and enabled me to help others: my master's degree allowed me to move beyond the youth centre and to teach addictions counselling.

Context is important to process the concept of flourishing in a meaningful, practical way. Real-life examples help. You can be flourishing in one area and not others. To an onlooker, it might seem like you have everything, but you still feel empty inside. Having money, education, and a good job will not, in and of itself, bring happiness. You can spend all your time and energy on your money level and flourish there, but at what cost? Have other levels been neglected?

Researchers have found that people who are in tune with psychological flourishing are more likely to experience higher boosts in positive emotions in response to everyday events. These boosts have a cumulative effect and result in greater opportunities for flourishing over time.[11]

But the challenge is that life isn't all good or all bad. If we improve on one level and get to the point of flourishing, there may be unintended consequences. For example, my quest for learning and my career affected my personal relationships; I didn't have as much time, focus, or energy to pursue and maintain them. My need to learn trumped most things. I'm now at a point where I can see the whole life pillar and understand the importance of stepping back, looking at each level, and determining the barriers or gaps that may be impacting me or preventing me from finding the happiness I want.

Just like working on building blocks in each level can bring you closer toward mental health, fear, failure, focus, and finishing are the building blocks of flourishing. But building blocks can topple if you don't maintain them. Even if your money level is arranged to your liking, it still requires daily housekeeping to ensure it remains in that condition. Getting to this stage doesn't mean you can rest on your laurels. Flourishing for life ultimately requires self-monitoring and tracking to ensure that you're doing what needs to be done to maintain each level to your desired standards.

> "Everybody wants to build and nobody wants to do maintenance."
>
> KURT VONNEGUT

## Try Not to Overdo It

When you put your focus on one area of life at the expense of others, you can develop tunnel vision. Too many of us are living in a state of acute health risk; we continue to push until something could break—or does. When you push yourself through discomfort, you can ignore the signs that it's time to slow down or stop.

If you're working, a key area you can self-monitor is the career level. Work consumes a large percentage of our time. For some of us, it takes over and becomes our life. When work becomes the only facet of life in which you are flourishing, it can be extremely destructive.

For some people, the repeated focus on work can, if not managed, evolve into an addictive disorder: workaholism.

They're in danger of over-flourishing in this one level at the cost of flourishing in life. A workaholic is trying to get their self-worth from their job. Why? Because their perception is that it gives them more internal reward than home life or social interactions.[12] Like drug addicts, people addicted to work develop negative habits to maintain their high, the adrenaline rush they get from work. They're internally driven to focus on their work for long periods of time. It's common for them to have obsessive-compulsive tendencies about work, and they often use their job to escape from the world outside of work.

Too much work at the expense of other levels can put you at risk. I find that many people are on autopilot when it comes to work. Whether they're at risk for a work addiction or burn-out, their days and months fly by without a lot of purpose or clarity on what they really want, other than money to pay their bills. To create happiness, you need to feel that you're in control of what you can control.

Investing too much time in one of the five levels can be counterproductive to the welfare of the entire life pillar. I've experienced both work addiction and burnout. There was a period of my life when I was working sixty hours a week, doing two jobs to pay my bills and finance my education, as well as taking graduate courses. I hit the wall a few times, when I was so totally burned out that I had to take time off work or change my job to create a new beginning.

Even though I created the illusion for others that I knew what I was doing, on the inside things weren't right. I was anxious, I had difficulty sleeping, and I worried about way too many things because I was trying to do too many things, and all within the two levels of money and career.

Change comes in all shapes and forms. My wake-up call came when I turned fifty and was diagnosed with a non-cancerous brain tumour. This significant life event made me pause and think about why I was working so hard. It was at that point that I said to myself, "I have enough education; I can use this time for other things in life." Shortly afterward, my father passed away. I realized that I was flourishing in many areas, but I was making a common mistake. I kept moving the goal posts and wanted to do more.

I realized that to enjoy life, I had to focus more energy on my relationships and personal health. Both areas may have appeared to the world as flourishing, but to be honest, I wasn't focused on them enough. It wasn't until I was honest with myself, started to pay more attention, and made personal decisions to redirect energy toward my health and relationships that I was able to feel more total wellness and happiness. It's easy to stick to a comfortable routine and accept what's not working. But hiding in one area of your life is an excuse not to focus on other areas.

I'm becoming more committed to repositioning my life so that I can put more focus on my personal relationships and health. And in time, I suspect that with focus I'll be able to set goals that will get me on track to flourishing. However, I know it will take time, and with this knowledge I can be patient and enjoy the process rather than feel pressure. I know what the F-it process will bring if I pay attention to where I am and what I'm doing.

I've learned that NOW is the only thing we can control. I use this simple acronym to remind myself what this means:

**N**othing we want in life happens until we decide to change what we're doing.

**O**pen to the possibility that others may have the information we need, we can ask others for insights that might spark creativity and help determine where to start.

**W**hat we really want and why we want it: to flourish we'll benefit from having a clear mental picture of what flourishing is and what it means to achieve it.

My early mistake was not allowing myself to enjoy my accomplishments, as I was always focused on the next task. I'm learning that it doesn't matter what the outside world thinks. In the end, we need to make our own decisions about whether what we're doing is enough. Today, I get a great sense of pride every time I pull into my driveway and see my valley bulldogs come to meet me and escort me into my home, where I can catch up with family and friends and share stories of the day.

I'm still a work in progress. But by adopting the *F*-it process I've learned how to stop hiding and start living, taking chances to increase my overall happiness. It's not always perfect and I experience setbacks, but it's much more enjoyable than not trying at all. As long as we're living, we're evolving, provided we're aware, accountable, and willing to act.

Many of us are typically somewhere in the middle, focusing on an area of life or just starting to make gains. We may not be flourishing, but we certainly aren't failing. If we're trying to eat better, and we pay attention to just fourteen of the twenty-one meals in a typical week, does that mean we're failing? Of course not. We're doing better than someone who doesn't focus at all. We need to give ourselves a break as we move through the process, as we may never get to perfection. The quest of trying can help us get closer over time to our target goals and sense that we're flourishing. Small changes can have a major impact on our overall sense of well-being.

Flourishing is good medicine for your mental health. Be clear on what levels of your life pillar are flourishing and what levels you would like to see improved. As you focus on improving areas of your life, keep in mind the benefits for maintaining the areas where you're currently flourishing. Don't take things you've accomplished for granted. Once you learn how to flourish in one or more levels, keep practising what got you to this point.

## Maintain Flourishing

Keep in mind that flourishing isn't about perfection; it's about feeling you've achieved a desired level and that what seemed hard now seems easier and possible. Maintaining a flourishing state requires a commitment to monitoring and measuring progress to ensure you stay on track. Being honest with yourself with respect to where you are and what you're doing can be the best way of moving forward.

Sometimes this requires engaging in daily behaviours like physical activity to maintain your fitness level, or monitoring your financials on a weekly basis. It helps to be aware of what maintenance steps are required and what expectations you are setting for yourself to maintain your flourishing. Even if you're not flourishing in all areas yet, it can help to be mindful of what you're doing to maintain each level. That way, you can condition your mind to be focused on what you need to do daily and weekly to flourish.

Using a journal, create your own Flourishing Weekly Checklist. You can use this sample checklist as a model.

| Five Levels | Example: does not need much detail, just be clear what actions you are consciously committing to each day |
| --- | --- |
| Money | ☐ Pay off credit card each month |
| Career | ☐ Have a short meeting with my project manager about daily tasks |
| Relationships | ☐ Protect date night<br>☐ Text mother to see how she's doing |
| Physical Health | ☐ Get minimum of seven hours sleep<br>☐ Monitor weight |
| Mental Health | ☐ Complete daily journal<br>☐ Meditate five minutes a day |

## Flourishing for Life

Flourishing is not really an outcome; it's more a state of mind. The more you believe you're flourishing, the better your mental health will be and the healthier and happier you'll be—as will the people in your life.

Like most people, I have good days and challenging ones. I've learned that I can increase my opportunities for good days by paying attention to how well I'm doing in each of my five levels. I know that there's no need for me to settle if I believe I can flourish more.

Flourishing is a wonderful feeling when you know you've achieved something you want, as well as when you know you're helping other people. When I read of folks like Bill Gates and Warren Buffett committing billions of dollars to noble causes so their wealth can help others, I believe this is evidence that they're flourishing with respect to their money. I don't need to be a billionaire to get the same feeling, whether by helping someone who is down on their potential, supporting a foster child, or many other acts. What I'm saying by my actions is that I have enough money and am sharing surplus to help others.

Regardless of what level you're focusing on, you can help others at work, at home, or in your communities when you feel you're flourishing and believe you have the capacity to give. This act becomes a fuel that powers many successful and happy people. Finding more happiness is about looking at your life and assessing what you can control.

My motivation to write this book was to share a process that I've used personally and with many individuals. It's helpful to have a map to get from point *A* to point *B* when you're not sure where to turn. To not have a frame of reference or clarity on what you can control and what you can do to find happiness and well-being can be frightening and fuel hopelessness.

Once you complete the book and start to shape up levels that need attention, I encourage you to track your progress every ninety days to help you stay focused on what you want your well-being and mental health to be.

As you see some progress in a building block and level, you might want to move on to another block or level. Assess your flourishing summary so you know where to concentrate. For each level put a check mark.

|  | Fear | Failure | Focus | Finishing | Flourishing |
|---|---|---|---|---|---|
| Money |  |  |  |  |  |
| Career |  |  |  |  |  |
| Relation- ships |  |  |  |  |  |
| Physical Health |  |  |  |  |  |
| Mental Health |  |  |  |  |  |

Life is busy, and it's easy to get distracted. The levels where you've scored the lowest may be the areas that are impacting the quality of life you're currently experiencing. The *F*-it process is dynamic; it doesn't go just one way and you're done. Once you get one level sorted and in order, you can't ignore it if you want to continue to flourish.

Life deals us all a set of cards, and our environment can be both positive and negative for our development and happiness. The more you know about each step, the better you can move from chance to intention—and from fear to flourishing.

Today, when I'm upset about anything, I use the *F*-it model to help me diagnose and self-correct. Through awareness, I can determine what is and is not working for me. You're accountable for what you can control, and nothing typically changes or improves in life until you act.

I've learned that I—more than anyone or anything else— impact my happiness and well-being. That's good news, because in the end all I have control over is myself. Perhaps you'll come to the same conclusion about yourself today or one day soon—if you haven't already.

Learning is a lifelong process that's never completed. It's not all about grades and school; it's about learning how to get along in a job to pay bills, how to get along with others, and how to define what's important for you. Learning to believe in myself, in my potential and my worth, was the biggest lesson of all. It was the launch pad for everything that followed.

We all need to define success on our own terms. Being healthy and happy clearly is not intuitive. If that were the case, we wouldn't have as much ill health as we do. The good news is that we can be taught how to flourish. We can choose happiness. We just need to be willing to make the effort.

# ACKNOWLEDGEMENTS

ALL MY ACADIA professors and coaches took the time to help me learn. If not for their kindness and willingness to find potential in me, I could not have written this book and would not be where I am in my career. Those caring professionals assumed the role that my mother had instinctively filled when I was in elementary school. Their generosity of spirit is what moved me to share what I've learned.

Few of us can do it alone, and seldom do we need to. What I learned at Acadia is that it's perfectly fine to ask for help. I have no shame in sharing with my employer and peers that I have a mental illness that impacts the way I read and write, as well as my concentration and focus. I developed the confidence to be a walking, talking accommodation. I know that for the rest of my life I will never be able to write a sentence without an editor correcting it or trying to figure out what I'm saying. So what? I don't have to be able to do things perfectly. I just need to share my thinking, and I welcome support from others. When I'm feeling lost or down, writing becomes my cure—no stress, no strain. When I complete a book, I get the sense that I'm flourishing, fulfilling my life purpose: to help others learn how to reach their full potential by lowering their risk for developing chronic diseases or mental health issues.

To those Acadia University professors and coaches who took the time to help me learn how to learn. If not for their kindness and willingness to find the potential in me, I would not have developed the confidence to believe I could do the work I do today. Without them, I would not have written this book.

To my mom, because without her I never would have made it to Acadia.

I must recognize Al Kingsbury, who has edited pretty much every article, book, paper, thesis, and blog I have written over the past twenty-five years. I am blessed to have found the right people at the right time in my life, who helped me fulfill my personal *why*: to help people discover their potential and then learn how to realize it.

# NOTES

## Introduction: Start Living

1   My thinking on this process was influenced by Carol Ryff's model
of psychological well-being. (Carol Ryff, "Happiness Is Everything,
or Is It? Explorations on the Meaning of Psychological Well-Being,"
*Journal of Personality and Social Psychology* 57, no. 6 (1989): 1069–
81.) This model suggests that observable behaviours can predict our
happiness and psychological well-being—the antithesis of strain.
Ryff's research found that how effectively each of us can manage
our perceived day-to-day stressors influences our psychological
well-being, which can be measured using the following six scales:

· Self-acceptance: maintaining a positive attitude toward oneself and
one's past life
· Positive relations with others: creating high-quality, satisfying
relationships
· Autonomy: having a sense of self-determination, independence,
and freedom from norms
· Purpose in life: having life goals with a defined purpose

- Environmental mastery: the ability to manage life and one's surroundings
- Personal growth: being open to new experiences and ongoing personal growth

The key behind Ryff's work is to achieve a desired outcome, requiring focus and action.

2. Many people confuse *mental health* with *mental illness.*

*Mental health* is defined as a state of well-being necessary for an individual to realize their own potential, where they can cope with and learn from the everyday stresses of life, can work productively and fruitfully, and are able to contribute to their community. ("Mental Health: A State of Well-being," World Health Organization, http://www.who.int/features/factfiles/mental_health/en/.) By contrast, *mental illness* is defined as a large collection of medically defined disorders that affect a person's mood, thinking, and/or behaviour.

Mental illness impacts all ages, educational levels, incomes, and cultures—one out of five people in Canada has a mental health concern. ("Fast Facts about Mental Illness," Canadian Mental Health Association, http://www.cmha.ca/media/fast-facts-about-mental-illness/.) People who aren't able to manage their mental health and get out of a negative cycle are at risk for developing a mental illness. Not all mental illnesses are genetic; some originate from gaps in one's ability to cope with psychosocial stress. Mental illness also includes all forms of addictive behaviours. Mental illness often manifests before a person turns eighteen, whether the root cause is genetic or psychosocial. ("Child and Youth Mental Health," Canadian Teachers' Federation, https://www.ctf-fce.ca/Research-Library/HillDay2013_MentalHealth.pdf.) Sociologist and psychologist Corey Keyes suggests that mental health problems and happiness/well-being are not a part of the same continuum. (Corey L. Keyes, "Mental Illness and/or Mental Health?: Investigating Axioms of the Complete State Model of Health," *Journal of Consulting and Clinical Psychology* 73, no. 3 (2005): 539.) For example, a person can have a severe mental illness and still have good mental health.

Whether you have a mental illness or not, you are accountable for nurturing your mental health. One key way of doing this is by managing stress—whether perceived or real.

Mental illness conditions range from mild to severe. Some types are referred to as organic, which includes neurological disorders—ADHD, learning disabilities, schizophrenia, and bipolar disorder, for instance. They originate from birth and their impact shows up at different developmental stages. Other types, like post-traumatic stress disorder (PTSD), can occur due to exposure to trauma or to lifestyle choices that lead to addictive disorders. They can also result from gaps in coping skills that determine how effectively one copes with psychosocial stress.

3   The five levels were inspired by Alfred Adler's original five life tasks, discussed in chapter four, as well as Abraham Maslow's Hierarchy of Needs.

4   See, for example, Martin E.P. Seligman, *Flourish: A Visionary New Understanding of Happiness and Well-being* (New York: Free Press, 2011).

5   Shawn Achor, *Before Happiness: The 5 Hidden Keys to Achieving Success, Spreading Happiness, and Sustaining Positive Change* (New York: Crown Publishing, 2013).

## Chapter 1: Own Your Story

1   Bill Howatt, "Learn to Calm Your Stressed Mind with Visualization," *Globe and Mail*, December 8, 2016, https://www.theglobeand mail.com/report-on-business/careers/workplace-award/learn-to -calm-your-stressed-mind-with-visualization/article33241100/.

2   William J. Long, "Quantum Theory and Neuroplasticity: Implications for Social Theory," *Journal of Theoretical and Philosophical Psychology* 26, no. 1–2 (2006): 78–94.

3 As I discussed in: William Howatt, *The Coping Crisis: Discover Why Coping Skills Are Required for a Healthy & Fulfilling Life* (Toronto: Morneau Shepell, 2015).

## Chapter 2: Good Stress vs. Bad Stress

1 Roman Kupriyanov and Renad Zhdanov, "The Eustress Concept: Problems and Outlooks," *World Journal of Medical Sciences* 11, no. 2 (2014): 179–85.

2 Francesco Marcatto et al., "Work-Related Stress Risk Factors and Health Outcomes in Public Sector Employees," *Safety Science* 89 (2016): 274–8.

3 Julienne E. Bower, Judith Tedlie Moskowitz, and Elissa Epel, "Is Benefit Finding Good for Your Health?: Pathways Linking Positive Life Changes after Stress and Physical Health Outcomes," *Current Directions in Psychological Science* 18, no. 6 (2009): 337–41.

4 Richard S. Lazarus, "From Psychology Stress to the Emotions: A History of Changing Outlooks," *Annual Review of Psychology* 44 (1993): 1–21.

5 Andrew Denovan and Ann Macaskill, "Stress and Subjective Well-being among First Year UK Undergraduate Students," *Journal of Happiness Studies* 18, no. 2 (2017): 505–25.

## Chapter 3: Assess Your Living Situation

1 Joseph E. McGrath, and Fraziska Tschan, "Time, Stress, and Coping Processes" in *Temporal Matters in Social Psychology: Examining the Role of Time in the Lives of Groups and Individuals*, ed. McGrath and Tschan (Washington, DC: American Psychological Association, 2004), 69–98.

## Chapter 4: Fear

1 Guy Winch, "Why Rejection Hurts So Much—and What to Do about It," *TED Ideas*, December 8, 2015, http://ideas.ted.com/why-rejection-hurts-so-much-and-what-to-do-about-it/.

2 Ethan Kross et al., "Social Rejection Shares Somatosensory Representations with Physical Pain," *Proceedings of the National Academy of Sciences of the United States of America*, 2011, http://www.pnas.org/content/108/15/6270.full.pdf.

3 Guy Winch, "Ten Surprising Facts about Rejection," *Psychology Today*, July 3, 2013, https://www.psychologytoday.com/blog/the-squeaky-wheel/201307/10-surprising-facts-about-rejection.

4 Alfred Adler, *What Life Should Mean to You* (New York: Capricorn, 1958).

5 R. Plutchik and H.R. Conte, eds., *Circumplex Models of Personality and Emotions* (Washington, DC: American Psychological Association, 1997), 17–45.

6 These terms are often used interchangeably.

7 Albert Bandura, *Social Foundations of Thought and Action: A Social Cognitive Theory* (Englewood Cliffs, NJ: Prentice-Hall, 1986).

8 Helmut Altner et al., *Fundamentals of Sensory Physiology*, 3rd ed., ed. Robert F. Schmidt (New York: Springer, 1986), 116.

9 Extreme fear of failure is referred to as *atychiphobia* or *kakorrhaphiophobia*.

10 Walter B. Cannon, *Bodily Changes in Pain, Hunger, Fear and Rage: An Account of Recent Researches into the Function of Emotional Excitement* (New York: Appleton, 1915).

11  Vladimir M. Zatsiorsky, Mark Latash, and Fan Gao, "Unlike Robots, People Modulate Internal Forces during Object Manipulation," *WSEAS Transactions on Systems* 5, no. 12 (2006): 2801–3.

12  Sheldon Cohen et al., "Emotional Style and Susceptibility to the Common Cold," *Psychosomatic Medicine* 65, no. 4 (2003): 652–7.

13  Doc Childre and Deborah Rozman, *Transforming Depression: The HeartMath Solution to Feeling Overwhelmed, Sad, and Stressed* (Oakland, CA: New Harbinger Publications, 2007).

14  Aaron T. Beck, Gary Brown, and Robert A. Steer, "Prediction of Eventual Suicide in Psychiatric Inpatients by Clinical Ratings of Hopelessness," *Journal of Consulting and Clinical Psychology* 57, no. 2 (1989): 309–10.

15  Katie Hanson, "What Exactly Is Hope and How Can You Measure It?," *Positive Psychology*, October 24, 2009, http://positive psychology.org.uk/hope-theory-snyder-adult-scale/.

16  Philip Brickman, Dan Coates, and Ronnie Janoff-Bulman, "Lottery Winners and Accident Victims: Is Happiness Relative?," *Journal of Personality and Social Psychology* 36, no. 8 (1978): 917–27.

17  Sonya Lyubomirsky, Laura King, and Ed Diener, "The Benefits of Frequent Positive Affect: Does Happiness Lead to Success?," *Psychological Bulletin* 131, no. 6 (2005): 803–55.

18  Stephanie L. Simon-Dack, and Cheri L. Marmarosh, "Neurosciences and Adult Health Behaviors: Recent Findings and Implications for Counseling Psychology," *Journal of Counseling Psychology* 61, no. 4 (2014): 528–33.

19  Dawson Church, *The Genie in Your Genes: Epigenetic Medicine and the New Biology of Intention* (Fulton, CA: Elite Books, 2007); Gian Vittorio Caprara and Patrizia Steca, "Affective and Social Self-regulatory Efficacy Beliefs as Determinants of Positive Thinking and Happiness," *European Psychologist* 10, no. 4 (2005): 275–86.

20 Joseph Hayes, Cindy L.P. Ward, and Ian McGregor, "Why Bother? Death, Failure, and Fatalistic Withdrawal from Life," *Journal of Personality and Social Psychology* 110, no. 1 (2016): 96–115.

21 Salvatore R. Maddi, "The Courage and Strategies of Hardiness as Helpful in Growing Despite Major, Disruptive Stresses," *American Psychologist* 63, no. 6 (2008): 563–4.

## Chapter 5: Failure

1 Joseph P. Forgas, "On Being Happy and Mistaken: Mood Effects on the Fundamental Attribution Error," *Journal of Personality and Social Psychology* 75, no. 2 (1998): 318–31.

2 Lisa K. Libby, Greta Valenti, Alison Pfent, and Richard P. Eibach, "Seeing Failure in Your Life: Imagery Perspective Determines whether Self-esteem Shapes Reactions to Recalled and Imagined Failure," *Journal of Personality and Social Psychology* 101, no. 6 (2011): 1157–73.

3 Steven F. Maier and Martin E.P. Seligman, "Learned Helplessness at Fifty: Insights from Neuroscience," *Psychological Review* 123, no. 4 (2016): 349–67.

4 Deborah Stipek, *Motivation to Learn* (Boston: Allyn & Bacon: 1988).

5 Leon Festinger, *A Theory of Cognitive Dissonance* (Stanford, CA: Stanford University Press, 1957).

6 Jack W. Kostal, Nathan R. Kuncel, and Paul R. Sackett, "Grade Inflation Marches On: Grade Increases from the 1990s to 2000s," *Educational Measurement: Issues and Practice* 35, no. 1 (2016): 11–20.

7 Gervase R. Bushe, "The Appreciative Inquiry Model," in *The Encyclopedia of Management Theory*, ed. Eric H. Kessler (Sage Publications, 2013).

8   Kristen D. Neff, "The Development and Validation of a Scale to Measure Self-compassion," *Self and Identity* 2 (2003): 223-50.

9   Albert Bandura, *Social Learning Theory* (Englewood Cliffs, NJ: Prentice-Hall, 1977).

10  Sarah-Jeanne Salvy, Kayla de la Haye, Julie C. Bowker, and Roel C.J. Hermans, "Influence of Peers and Friends on Children's and Adolescents' Eating and Activity Behaviors," *Physiological Behavior* 106, no. 3: 369-78.

## Chapter 6: Focus

1   Ross E. O'Hara, Stephen Armeli, Marcella H. Boynton, and Howard Tennen, "Emotional Stress-Reactivity and Positive Affect among College Students: The Role of Depression History," *Emotion* 14, no. 1 (2014): 193-202.

2   Nick Levine, "The Nature of the Glut: Information Overload in Postwar America," *History of the Human Sciences* 30, no. 1 (2017): 32-49.

3   Yuichi Sasaki, Daisuke Kawai, and Satoshi Kitamura, "Unfriend or Ignore Tweets?: A Time Series Analysis on Japanese Twitter Users Suffering from Information Overload," *Computers in Human Behavior* 64 (2016): 914-22.

4   Bobby Swar, Tahir Hameed, and Iris Reychav, "Information Overload, Psychological Ill-being, and Behavioral Intention to Continue Online Healthcare Information Search," *Computers in Human Behavior* 70 (2017): 416-25.

5   L. Alison Phillips, Howard Leventhal, and Elaine A. Leventhal, "Assessing Theoretical Predictors of Long-Term Medication Adherence: Patients' Treatment-Related Beliefs, Experiential Feedback and Habit Development," *Psychology & Health* 28 (2013): 1135-51.

6   Amelie U. Wiedemann, Benjamin Gardner, Nina Knoll, and Silke Burkert, "Intrinsic Rewards, Fruit and Vegetable Consumption, and Habit Strength: A Three-Wave Study Testing the Associative-Cybernetic Model," *Applied Psychology: Health and Well-Being 6*, no. 1 (2014): 119–34.

7   D. Katz, "Positive Reflections: Purpose Changes Everything," *Lesbian News* 42, no. 11 (2017): 56–58.

8   Piers Steel and Joseph R. Ferrari, "Sex, Education and Procrastination: An Epidemiological Study of Procrastinators' Characteristics from a Global Sample," *European Journal of Personality* 27, no. 1 (2013): 51–58.

9   Carol D. Ryff and Corey Lee M. Keyes, "The Structure of Psychological Well-being Revisited," *Journal of Personality and Social Psychology* 69, no. 4 (1995): 719–27.

10  Patrick L. Hill and Nicholas A. Turiano, "Purpose in Life as a Predictor of Mortality across Adulthood," *Psychological Science* 25, no. 7 (2014): 1482–6.

11  William Magee, "Effects of Gender and Age on Pride in Work, and Job Satisfaction," *Journal of Happiness Studies* 16, no. 5 (2015): 1091–115.

12  Mihaly Csikszentmihalyi, *Creativity: Flow and the Psychology of Discovery and Invention* (New York: HarperCollins, 1996); *Finding Flow: The Psychology of Engagement with Everyday Life* (New York: BasicBooks, 1997).

13  Mihaly Csikszentmihalyi, *The Evolving Self: A Psychology for the Third Millennium* (New York: HarperCollins, 1993).

14  Jerome Seymour Bruner, *Toward a Theory of Instruction* (Cambridge, MA: Belknap, 1996).

15  Paul J. Silvia and Todd B. Kashdan, "Interesting Things and Curious People: Exploration and Engagement as Transient States and Enduring Strengths," *Social Psychology and Personality Compass* 3, no. 5 (2009): 785–97.

## Chapter 7: Finishing

1  Howard Gardner, *Multiple Intelligences: The Theory in Practice* (New York: Basic, 1983).

2  Bill Howatt, "Supporting Employees to Make Behavioural Change," Morneau Shepell white paper, 2017.

3  M. Robin DiMatteo and Kelly B. Haskard, "Further Challenges in Adherence Research: Measurements, Methodologies, and Mental Health Care," *Medical Care* 44, no. 4 (April 2006): 297–9.

4  Joyce P. Yi et al., "The Role of Resilience on Psychological Adjustment and Physical Health in Patients with Diabetes," *British Journal of Health Psychology* 13, no. 2 (2008): 311–25.

## Chapter 8: Flourishing

1  Kenneth Nowack, "Facilitating Successful Behavior Change: Beyond Goal Setting to Goal Flourishing," *Consulting Psychology Journal: Practice and Research* 69, no. 3 (2017): 153–71.

2  S. Katherine Nelson, Kristin Layous, Steven W. Cole, and Sonja Lyubomirsky, "Do unto Others or Treat Yourself?: The Effects of Prosocial and Self-Focused Behavior on Psychological Flourishing," *Emotion* 16, no. 6 (2016): 850–61.

3  Joseph Chancellor, Seth Margolis, and Sonja Lyubomirsky, "The Propagation of Everyday Prosociality in the Workplace," *Journal of Positive Psychology* 13, no. 3 (2018): 271–83.

4   Corey L.M. Keyes, "Chronic Physical Conditions and Aging: Is Mental Health a Potential Protective Factor?," *Ageing International* 30, no. 1 (2005): 88–104.

5   Corey L.M. Keyes, "Promoting and Protecting Mental Health as Flourishing: A Complementary Strategy for Improving National Mental Health," *American Psychologist* 62, no. 2 (2007): 95–108.

6   Jennifer R. Dunn and Maurice E. Schweitzer, "Feeling and Believing: The Influence of Emotion on Trust," *Journal of Personality and Social Psychology* 88, no. 5 (2005): 736–74.

7   Keyes, "Chronic Physical Conditions and Aging."

8   Nelson, Layous, Cole, and Lyubomirsky, "Do unto Others or Treat Yourself?"

9   Richard M. Ryan and Edward L. Deci, "On Happiness and Human Potentials: A Review of Research on Hedonic and Eudaimonic Well-being," *Annual Review of Psychology* 52 (2001): 141–66.

10  Aristotle, *Nicomachean Ethics*, trans. Martin Ostwald (Upper Saddle River, NJ: Prentice Hall, 1999).

11  Lahnna I. Catalino and Barbara L. Fredrickson, "A Tuesday in the Life of a Flourisher: The Role of Positive Emotional Reactivity in Optimal Mental Health," *Emotion* 11, no. 4 (2011): 938–50.

12  Marilyn Machlowitz, *Workaholics: Living with Them, Working with Them* (Reading, MA: Addison-Wesley, 1980).

# INDEX

Csikszentmihalyi, Mihaly, 110
curiosity, 116

debt, 4–5, 7, 66
discouragement, 47, 55
disgust, 48
distress, 27–28. *See also* stress
dyslexia, 9, 24, 49, 100, 109, 118

education, 7, 34, 47
Ellis, Albert, 82
emotional refractory period,
    96–97
emotional well-being, positive,
    143
emotions, 45, 48. *See also* fear;
    grief; happiness; stress
environment, 50, 73, 157n1
epigenetics, 60
eudaimonic well-being, 143
eustress, 27. *See also* stress
external locus of control (ELOC),
    111–12

failure, 71–94; author's failure
    in grade two, 71–73, 93–94;
    effects of, 72–73; embracing
    failure, 83–84, 86–87; fail-
    ure loop, 28–29; fake failure,
    83; fear of, 48–50; focus on
    strengths and, 81–82; funda-
    mental attribution error and,
    73; grief as part of, 87–88;
    informed failure, 89; internal

and external support, 89–91;
    irrational thinking and,
    82–83; learned helplessness
    and, 75–76; learning curves
    and, 77–80; life satisfaction
    and, 91–93; moving from fear
    to, 55–56, 61; normalizing
    failure, 25, 47, 73–76, 79, 130;
    objective failure, 86; perma-
    nent failure, 89; and replaying
    accomplishments as a movie,
    80–81; self-compassion and,
    84; subjective failure, 85
fear, 43–66; author's experi-
    ence moving past, 62–65;
    author's public school strug-
    gles, 43–45, 46, 48–50, 51;
    choosing happiness, 58–61;
    deciding to move beyond,
    61–62, 65–66; of failure,
    48–50; fear traps, 54–55;
    fight-or-flight response,
    51–53; hope as antidote,
    56–58, 61, 62, 65; moving
    to failure from, 55–56, 61;
    Plutchik on, 48; of rejection,
    45–47; stress and, 27; that
    holds you back, 50–51
Festinger, Leon, 76
fight-or-flight response, 51–53, 54
finishing, 117–38; adherence
    and, 127; author's high school
    graduation, 117–19, 120–25;
    choosing goals with care,

money, 7, 34. *See also* debt
motivation, 29–30, 65, 90.
   *See also* conviction; hope;
   purpose

neurogenesis, 20
neuroplasticity, 20
NOW (acronym), 148

objective failure, 86
operant conditioning, 19–20
optimism, 61
over-generalization, 83

perfection, 84
permanent failure, 89
persistence, 132–33
personal growth, 65–66, 76, 81,
   157n1
physical health, 7, 34
Plutchik, Robert, 48
positive, accentuation of, 19–21,
   81–82
positive psychology, 11
psychological functioning,
   positive, 143
psychological well-being, 157n1
purpose, 104–9, 157n1. *See also*
   conviction

rejection, 45–47
relationships, 7, 34, 157n1
resiliency: building reserves
   of, 127, 132–34; definition,

10; for finishing, 125; goal of,
142; risks from lack of, 10;
from success and happiness,
39, 59; total wellness and,
134–35. *See also* coping skills
Ryff, Carol, 108, 157n1

sadness, 48
self-acceptance, 47, 143, 157n1
self-compassion, 84, 138
self-criticism, 83, 85
self-labelling, 83
skills, mastery of, 90
Snyder, Charles Richard, 58
social advancement, 77
social functioning, positive, 143
spiritual dimension, 47
story, owning your, 17–25;
   accentuating the positive,
   19–21; changing your story,
   23–25; mental map, 21–23;
   oldest memory, 17–19
strengths, focus on, 81–82
stress, 27–32; affect polarization and, 96; effects of bad
   stress, 28–29; effects on finishing, 128; fear traps, 54–55;
   good vs. bad stress, 27–28;
   motivation from, 29–30; taking control of, 31–32
subjective failure, 85
success, 39, 80–81, 119–20, 153.
   *See also* failure; goal setting
suicide, 57

support, 89–91
surprise, 48

thin-slicing, 73–74
3C Model, the, 126–27, 129,
    130–31
total wellness, 7, 134–37
trust, 48
tunnel vision, 145

unknowing, 25

values, 141–42
Vonnegut, Kurt, 145

well-being: emotional, 143;
    eudaimonic, 143; hedonic, 143;
    psychological, 157n1; total
    wellness, 7, 134–37. *See also*
    happiness
work, 47. *See also* career
workaholism, 145–46

Zatsiorsky, Vladimir, 52
zone, being in the, 110–11

# ABOUT THE AUTHOR

BILL HOWATT IS Ph.D., Ed.D., Post Doctorate Behavioral Science, University of California, Los Angeles, Semel Institute for Neuroscience and Human Behavior, RTC, RSW, ICADC. He is the President of Howatt HR and is also currently the Chief of Research, Workforce Productivity at The Conference Board of Canada, leading the Board's applied research programs in workplace wellness, mental health, and workforce productivity. Prior to joining The Conference Board in 2018, Dr. Howatt worked as Chief of Research and Development, Workforce Productivity at Morneau Shepell, where he launched a total health consulting strategy designed to improve health engagement and productivity in Canadian organizations.

Dr. Howatt is known as one of Canada's top experts in mental health issues in the workplace and has more than thirty years' experience in the field of mental health, addiction, and human resources consulting. As a highly respected columnist for the *Globe and Mail*, author, clinician, consultant, and speaker, he effortlessly engages and inspires both individuals and groups.

Dr. Howatt is the Chair of CSA Standard Z1008: Management of Substance Related Impairment in the Workplace. He is the creator of the online Certificate in Management Essentials program, a Senate-approved leaders program that offers eighteen courses through the University of New Brunswick. He is also the creator of Pathway to Coping, an online course at the same university that is grounded in the cognitive-behavioural therapy approach, and an online course on cannabis for employees and leaders.

Dr. Howatt has published numerous books and articles, such as *The Coping Crisis*, *Pathway to Coping*, the Wiley Series on addictions, *The Human Services Counseling Toolbox*, and *The Addiction Counselor's Desk Reference*. He is a regular contributor to the *Globe and Mail* 9 to 5 and Leadership Lab columns and *The Chronicle Herald*.

**www.howatthr.com**